P.G. WODEHOUSE

Pelham ('Plum') Grenville Wodehouse was born in Guildford in 1881. After leaving school he spent two years as a banker, before switching careers to sports reporter and columnist at the *Globe* newspaper. Around this time he started writing short stories, mainly for boys' magazine *The Captain*, before discovering his talent for comic dialogue. By 1910 he was reaching millions of readers all over the world, and dividing his time between his homes in the US, France and Britain.

In his ninety-six years he wrote almost two hundred short stories, plays, articles, song lyrics – including working with Cole Porter on the musical *Anything Goes* – and novels. He began writing the Jeeves and Wooster novels, for which he is best known, with *The Man with Two Left Feet* in 1917, followed by others such as *Right Ho, Jeeves* (1934), *The Code of the Woosters* (1938) and *Stiff Upper Lip, Jeeves* (1963), and finally *Aunts Aren't Gentlemen* in 1974.

His final years saw him constantly in and out of hospitals with a series of illnesses. He continued writing throughout, leaving his final work, *Sunset at Blandings*, unfinished. He died of a heart attack in a hospital in Southampton, Long Island, on Valentine's Day 1975.

THE GOODALE BROTHERS

Like many siblings growing up together, writers Robert and David Goodale enjoyed their own, very particular brand of humour. As children they created a range of ridiculous characters that seamlessly evolved into members of their extended family. It was only later that they discovered that P.G. Wodehouse had beaten them to it, in creating an entirely credible world full of even more deliciously bonkers characters.

As adults entering the real world, Robert became an actor, while David pursued a career as a documentary film-maker, but both remained committed to making people laugh. In 2010 they were encouraged to combine their comic talents to adapt P.G. Wodehouse's *The Code of the Woosters* for the stage. They finally put pen to paper, and several drafts later, with the blessing of the Wodehouse Estate, *Perfect Nonsense* was born.

JEEVES AND WOOSTER
in
PERFECT NONSENSE

A new play from the works of
P.G. Wodehouse

by
The Goodale Brothers

NICK HERN BOOKS
London
www.nickhernbooks.co.uk

A Nick Hern Book

Jeeves and Wooster in 'Perfect Nonsense' first published in Great Britain in 2014 as a paperback original by Nick Hern Books Limited, The Glasshouse, 49a Goldhawk Road, London W12 8QP

Jeeves and Wooster in 'Perfect Nonsense' copyright © 2014 Robert Goodale and David Goodale

Introduction copyright © 2014 Robert Goodale

Robert Goodale and David Goodale have asserted their right to be identified as the authors of this work

Cover image: Matthew Macfadyen as Jeeves and Stephen Mangan as Bertie; photography by Uli Weber, design by AKA

Designed and typeset by Nick Hern Books, London
Printed and bound in Great Britain by CPI Group (UK) Ltd

A CIP catalogue record for this book is available from the British Library

ISBN 978 1 84842 414 2

The Evolution of *Perfect Nonsense*
Robert Goodale

My first taste of P.G. Wodehouse came in my early twenties
when my twin brother and a mutual friend of ours used to quote
PGW phrases, sentences and extracts back and forth at each
other during late-night drinking sessions. I was never sure
whether it was the whisky, the Wodehouse or a combination of
the two that was making me laugh hysterically, but for years my
experience of the great man was confined to the blurry hours of
the night.

It was only when looking for material for a one-man show that I
picked up a Jeeves and Wooster book in the cold light of day
and realised what a comic genius Wodehouse really was. I also
discovered that some of his best material was being filtered
through the mouthpiece of Bertie Wooster. Here was a
storyteller, raconteur and vaudevillian performer who was
capable of charming any group of people into submission. Not
only was he a perfect frontman, but the characters who peopled
his world were gloriously eccentric, mad and passionate, all
with their bizarre and peculiar obsessions. Twenty pages into
Stiff Upper Lip, Jeeves and I knew that I had my one-man show.

The idea of indulging in a world where the loss of an objet d'art
from your silver collection was perceived as being a matter of
life and death could not have been more appealing. So I went
ahead and performed a couple of one-man shows based on this
material at the Edinburgh Festival and roped in my brother
David to direct *The Code of the Woosters*.

Twenty years later, the two of us were approached by Mark
Goucher to create another Wodehouse show, but on a larger
scale. It dawned on us that if we wanted to keep Bertie as the
raconteur we should write a play in which, encouraged by his
drinking pals, he would take over a West End theatre and
attempt to tell one of his stories in the form of a one-man show.
As his loyal valet, Jeeves would naturally accompany Bertie to

the theatre and, in the certain knowledge that the show was destined to go horribly wrong, he would have made certain contingency plans. The script almost wrote itself, and we revelled in the idea that the inscrutable and dignified Jeeves might draw on some hidden talents to play a number of the other characters.

We passed *Perfect Nonsense* on to Mark Goucher, did a reading of it for him and in turn the Wodehouse Estate, who gave it their blessing. The wonderfully inventive comedy director Sean Foley was then brought on board and his inspired suggestions, combined with Alice Power's brilliant ideas for the set design, helped raise the script to another level.

Although I had absolutely nothing to do with Stephen Mangan's or Matthew Macfadyen's involvement, I was thrilled when they were cast. Having worked with them both at the Royal Shakespeare Company, witnessed their extraordinary comic abilities and observed how well they got on together, there was no question in my mind as to how perfect a pairing they could be.

What was most gratifying about the whole process was that all of the above – along with Mark Hadfield (as Seppings) – were completely in tune with the conceit of the show and a lot of what was discovered in the rehearsal room found its way into the script. A true process of evolution, we like to think.

Jeeves and Wooster in 'Perfect Nonsense' was first presented in London at the Duke of York's Theatre on 30 October 2013 by Mark Goucher and Mark Rubinstein. The cast was as follows:

JEEVES	Matthew Macfadyen
BERTIE WOOSTER	Stephen Mangan
SEPPINGS	Mark Hadfield

Director	Sean Foley
Set and Costume Designer	Alice Power
Lighting Designer	James Farncombe
Sound Designer	Max and Ben Ringham
Casting Director	Sarah Bird CDG
Associate Director	Michael Gyngell
Associate Producer	Adam Blanshay
Associate Producer	Eleanor Lloyd

On 7 April 2014, the roles of Jeeves and Wooster were taken over by Mark Heap and Robert Webb respectively.

Characters

JEEVES, *played by himself*
BERTIE WOOSTER, *played by himself*
SEPPINGS, *played by himself*

SIR WATKYN BASSETT, *to be played by Jeeves*
GUSSIE FINK-NOTTLE, *to be played by Jeeves*
STIFFY BYNG, *to be played by Jeeves*
AUNT DAHLIA, *to be played by Seppings*
ANTIQUE-SHOP PROPRIETOR, *to be played by Seppings*
RODERICK SPODE, *to be played by Seppings*
BUTTERFIELD, *to be played by Seppings*
MADELINE BASSETT, *to be played by Seppings*
CONSTABLE OATES, *to be played by Seppings*

Note on the Text

When **BERTIE** *is written in bold, it is to indicate that he is talking directly to the audience.*

ACT ONE

Musical fanfare as curtain rises to reveal BERTIE WOOSTER, *dressed in black tie with a velvet smoking jacket, sitting in an armchair beside a standard lamp on an otherwise empty stage.* BERTIE *is looking down over his shoulder, tucking some notes away under the chair, apparently oblivious to the fact that he is now in full view of the audience. Suddenly, realising that all eyes are upon him, he checks his watch, and then looks out to the audience.*

BERTIE. I thought we said 7.30 for 8.00.

He stands up and addresses the audience.

What-ho! Now, the reason that I'm here, and you're there, is that I was at my club, the Drones the other night, and I was telling Bingo Little – you know Bingo – I was telling Bingo Little, in some detail, about a perfectly frightful weekend I recently spent at Totleigh Towers. And he said, 'Bertie, you should be doing this on the stage!' So, here I am... *Tout seul...* or as the French say, 'All on my own.' I mean, I've been to the theatre a couple of times, I've seen people act and have often thought, 'Well, how hard can that be?'

BERTIE *takes a deep breath and composes himself.*

So, here goes. Curtain up! Now, that's just a theatrical expression, of course, because the curtain has already gone up – otherwise you wouldn't be able to see me.

He strolls over to the armchair and sits down.

Now, the whole thing started when I was at home asleep in bed.

He leans back in the chair as if he is asleep and then suddenly sits bolt upright.

I woke.

He addresses an imaginary person beside him.

BERTIE. Jeeves!

BERTIE. I said.

He stands up and moves stage right in order to play the part of JEEVES.

Now, when I stand here I'll be playing the part of Jeeves.

BERTIE (*impersonating* JEEVES). Yes, sir.

BERTIE *returns to the seat to play himself again.*

BERTIE. And then I said:

BERTIE. If I had my life to live again, Jeeves, I would start it as an orphan without any aunts.

BERTIE *stands up and moves stage right again to assume the character of* JEEVES.

BERTIE. And then Jeeves said:

BERTIE (*impersonating* JEEVES). Indeed, sir.

BERTIE. And then I said:

BERTIE *returns to his seat to play himself again.*

BERTIE. Don't they put aunts in Turkey in sacks and drop...

BERTIE. No, hold on...

BERTIE *stands up, not knowing which part to play.*

And then Jeeves said. No – I said. No Jeeves said...

He stops and calls out to the real JEEVES.

BERTIE....Jeeves!

JEEVES *appears.*

JEEVES. Yes, sir.

BERTIE. Could you play Jeeves, Jeeves?

JEEVES. Certainly, sir.

BERTIE. Good. I can't keep that up all night. So, back to the story. It's a complex case of Gussie Fink-Nottle, Madeline Bassett, her father Sir Watkyn, her cousin Stiffy Byng, Roderick Spode and my Aunt Dahlia. Here we go. Your line, Jeeves.

JEEVES. Indeed, sir.

BERTIE. No, say your line, Jeeves.

JEEVES. Indeed, sir, is my line, sir.

BERTIE. Never mind. I'll start.

> BERTIE *resumes*.

Don't they put aunts in Turkey in sacks and drop them in the Bosphorus?

JEEVES. Odalisques, sir, I understand. Not aunts.

BERTIE. Well, why not aunts? Look at the trouble they cause in the world...

> BERTIE *suddenly breaks out of the dialogue and addresses the audience*.

BERTIE....No, wait... Hold the line a minute. I've gone off the rails. Would you believe it, I've started in the wrong place.

Right-ho. Let me start again. It really all began the day before the one you just saw me wake up in.

JEEVES. If you could allow me one moment, sir, I think we could set the scene somewhat more convincingly.

BERTIE. Well, I think it's pretty convincing already. You have to leave some things to the imagination, Jeeves.

> JEEVES *pulls on an art deco fireplace and places it centre stage*.

Jeeves, that is absolutely terrific!

> JEEVES *picks up two sticks and animates the flames of the fire*.

They're really getting their money's worth, aren't they?

JEEVES. They are indeed, sir.

JEEVES *hands* BERTIE *the sticks and then goes to open up a screen, stage left.*

BERTIE. It's a fire!

JEEVES. Perhaps you'd like to continue with your story.

BERTIE. Story?

JEEVES. In your pyjamas, sir.

JEEVES *points* BERTIE *towards the screen.*

BERTIE. Yes, of course, Jeeves.

BERTIE *goes behind the screen and calls out.*

Jeeves, get me one of those bracers of yours, will you?

BERTIE. I said, as I returned from the bathroom with that rather unpleasant feeling you get sometimes that you're going to die in about five minutes.

BERTIE *emerges from behind the screen, now dressed in pyjamas. He looks in amazement at his transformation before continuing.*

BERTIE. Jeeves! How are you doing this?

JEEVES. Your story, sir?

BERTIE. On the previous night. Not yesterday. In the story. I had given a little dinner at the Drones to my very good pal, Gussie Fink-Nottle. He was soon to be hitched to Madeline Bassett, only daughter of Sir Watkyn Bassett. Gussie was a shy and timid pal of mine who buried himself in the country and devoted himself entirely to the study of newts. But love will find a way, and he was now due to walk up the aisle with the ghastly girl. I call her a ghastly girl because she was a ghastly girl. A droopy, soupy, sentimental exhibit, with melting eyes and a cooing voice and the most extraordinary views on such things as stars and wabbits... rabbits.

JEEVES *pushes on a truck, which represents the wall behind the fireplace. Hanging directly above the mantelpiece is a framed picture.*

BERTIE. Good Lord, Jeeves. What's that?

JEEVES. It's called scenery, sir. It's quite widely used in the theatre.

BERTIE. Well, where did it come from?

JEEVES. When I learned of your intentions for this evening, sir, I took it upon myself to provide some suitable representations of relevant locations. Some of them are still under construction, sir.

BERTIE. For those of you who haven't been to my pad, this really does bear an uncanny resemblance to my...

JEEVES. Your story, sir.

BERTIE. Oh yes. Sorry.

BERTIE *sits down.*

BERTIE. Any post this morning, Jeeves?

BERTIE. I said, sitting nonchalantly.

JEEVES. Yes, sir. There is some literature from the travel bureau. I thought you might care to take a glance at it.

BERTIE. Oh? You did, did you? Jeeves, this nuisance must now cease.

JEEVES. Travel is highly educational, sir.

BERTIE. I can't do with any more education. I was full up years ago.

JEEVES. Very good, sir.

BERTIE. This round-the-world cruise that you want me to go on, Jeeves... You've become altogether too... Oh. What's the word?

JEEVES. I could not say, sir.

BERTIE. Pertinent? No, it's not pertinent. Pernicious? No it's not pernicious. It's on the tip of my tongue. Begins with a 'p' and means being a jolly sight too pushy. But it's not pushy.

JEEVES. Persistent, sir?

BERTIE. Persistent! That's the exact word I was after. Too persistent, Jeeves. Far too persistent.

JEEVES. Very good, sir.

BERTIE. Very good, Jeeves.

BERTIE *goes behind the screen to change.* JEEVES *places the tray on the mantelpiece and then brings on the jacket.*

Well, it was quite a satisfactory dinner at the Drones last night.

JEEVES. Indeed, sir.

BERTIE. Oh, most. An excellent time was had by all.

JEEVES. I trust there were not too many breakages, sir?

BERTIE. Not that I remember, Jeeves.

JEEVES. And I'm pleased to see that you were able to return in time for breakfast, sir.

BERTIE. Oh, yes.

JEEVES. It sounds as if you had a most enjoyable evening, sir?

BERTIE. Yes, can you stop asking me questions, Jeeves. I'm trying to get into this bally suit.

JEEVES. Indeed, sir.

BERTIE *sticks his head up from behind the screen.*

BERTIE. There are boring bits in every play and I'm afraid this is the one in mine.

BERTIE. Gussie sent his regards.

JEEVES. I appreciate the kind thought, sir. I trust Mr Fink-Nottle was in good spirits?

BERTIE. Extraordinarily good, considering the sands of time are running out and he will shortly have Sir Watkyn Bassett for a father-in-law. Sooner him than me, Jeeves, sooner him than me. Let's not forget, Jeeves, that…

BERTIE *appears from behind the folding screen, fully dressed except for his jacket, which* JEEVES *is holding.*

…he was the magistrate who fined me five pounds for pinching a policeman's helmet on Boat Race night.

JEEVES. Indeed, sir.

BERTIE. Any telephone communications this morning?

JEEVES. One, sir. From Mrs Travers.

BERTIE. Aunt Dahlia. Is she in town?

JEEVES. Yes, sir. She expressed a desire that you would ring her at your earliest convenience.

BERTIE. I will do even better. I will call in person.

JEEVES. Very good, sir.

JEEVES *snaps his fingers to cue the incidental music. A spotlight comes up to illuminate* BERTIE *as he attempts a mime-walk, while* JEEVES *rotates the fireplace and wall 180 degrees* (*transforming the set into* AUNT DAHLIA*'s library – although this is still in virtual darkness*). BERTIE *mime-walks, avoiding traffic and dogs.*

BERTIE. It was about half an hour's walk… I'll leave the rest of that to your imagination.

JEEVES, *who has reappeared, clicks his fingers to stop the music.*

BERTIE. Jeeves, how are you doing that?

BERTIE. So there I was at the Travers' residence, being greeted by old Seppings, Aunt Dahlia's butler.

BERTIE. Well, there's a problem, Jeeves. Who's going to play Seppings?

JEEVES. I had considered that eventuality, sir. I thought that Seppings might play himself, sir.

Enter SEPPINGS *bang on cue.*

SEPPINGS. Good evening, sir.

BERTIE. What are you doing here, Seppings?

SEPPINGS. I came to lend a hand, sir.

JEEVES. I was also going to suggest that we might call upon
Seppings to play a number of the other protagonists in this
re-enactment. He does have a particular aptitude for
impersonations.

SEPPINGS *coughs*.

BERTIE. Do you, Seppings?

SEPPINGS. I don't think I'm in a position to judge, sir.

BERTIE. Oh, jolly good. Well, this is all going rather
splendidly, isn't it?

JEEVES (*clearing his throat*). You were being 'Greeted by old
Seppings', sir.

BERTIE. Oh, yes.

JEEVES *exits, whilst* BERTIE *and* SEPPINGS *both take up
appropriate positions.*

BERTIE. Is Mrs Travers at home, Seppings?

SEPPINGS. Yes, sir. She has requested that she is not to be
disturbed this morning. But I do know that she wishes to
speak with you.

BERTIE. Yes, she does.

SEPPINGS. You will find her in the library... (*Realising that he
is already in 'the library'*.) shortly, sir.

BERTIE. Thank you, Seppings. That will be all.

SEPPINGS *exits.* BERTIE *strolls towards the wings.*

BERTIE. While I was waiting, I caught a glimpse of Uncle Tom
through the open door of the morning room. He was messing
about with his collection of old silver. The uncle is a bird
who, sighting a nephew, is apt to buttonhole him and become
a bit informative on the subject of silverware. Pull him away

from his love of perforated porringers and foliated sugar
shakers and he gets in such a state, he looks like something
that might have occurred to Ibsen in one of his less frivolous
moments. So I left him to himself and waited for Aunt Dahlia.

SEPPINGS *appears dressed as* AUNT DAHLIA.

DAHLIA. Hello, Bertie.

BERTIE. Seppings. That's terribly good.

BERTIE *breaks out into hysterics whilst* SEPPINGS *looks at him blankly.*

DAHLIA. You delirious old ass. What brings you here?

BERTIE *attempts to control himself and immerses himself back into the action.*

BERTIE. I understood, aged relative, that you wished to confer
with me.

DAHLIA. I didn't want you to come barging in, interrupting my
work. But I suppose some instinct must have told you that it
was my busy day.

BERTIE. If you were wondering if I could stay to lunch, have
no anxiety. I shall be delighted as always. What will Anatole
be giving us?

DAHLIA. Anatole won't be giving you anything. I'm
entertaining the novelist, Pomona Grindle...

BERTIE. She spoke as usual as if she was shouting across
ploughed fields in a high wind.

DAHLIA. So you were out on the tiles again last night.

BERTIE. What? Who told you that?

DAHLIA. It's an extraordinary thing – every time I see you,
you appear to be recovering from some debauch. Don't you
ever stop drinking? How about when you are asleep?

BERTIE. You wrong me, relative. Except at times of special
revelry, I am exceedingly moderate in my potations. A brace
of cocktails, a glass of wine at dinner and possibly a...

DAHLIA. Enough, Bertie, sit and listen. All I wanted was to tell you to go to an antique shop in the Brompton Road and sneer at a cow-creamer.

BERTIE. Do what to a what?

DAHLIA. They've got an eighteenth-century cow-creamer there that your Uncle Tom's going to buy this afternoon. It's a sort of cream jug, Bertie. It looks exactly like a cow, but smaller, of course, and made of silver. Go there and ask them to show it to you, and then sow doubts and misgivings in their mind and make them clip the price a bit. And tell them you think it's modern Dutch, which is apparently something a cow-creamer ought not to be… Understood? Good, because I've got work to do. Seppings, show Mr Wooster the door! (*Realising that 'SEPPINGS' is not available*.) Don't worry, Seppings, Mr Wooster can show himself out.

AUNT DAHLIA *exits*. BERTIE *positions himself downstage centre and starts mime-walking again*.

BERTIE. Oh, I'm going the wrong way. (*Turns and starts walking in the other direction*.) Many men might have been a bit put out at having their day cut into in this fashion, but scratch Bertram Wooster, I often say, and you find a Boy Scout. So I dutifully headed for the antique shop.

JEEVES *and* SEPPINGS *open up the bookshelves to reveal the counter of the antique shop*.

BERTIE. Is that supposed to represent the shop, Jeeves?

JEEVES. Perhaps I could recommend that if we refrained from drawing attention to the theatrical devices, it might make the narrative easier to follow.

JEEVES *rotates the handle adjacent to the picture frame and the sign for the antique shop is rolled into position*.

BERTIE. Oh, yes. Of course, Jeeves.

BERTIE *mimes entering the shop and* SEPPINGS *appears shortly afterwards as the* PROPRIETOR *and checks the display case*.

BERTIE. 'I say,' I began, entering; then paused as I perceived that the bloke in charge was attending to another customer and in spite of the poor light, was able to note that this other customer was no stranger to me.

SIR WATKYN BASSETT (*played by* JEEVES) *enters the shop under an open umbrella and inspects a cow-creamer that the* PROPRIETOR *is showing him.*

It was indeed Sir Watkyn Bassett in person. Himself. Not a picture. A weaker man, no doubt, would have tiptoed from the scene and headed for the horizon. But I stood firm.

JEEVES *turns to see* BERTIE.

BASSETT. Hullo, hullo. I know you, young man.

BERTIE. Oh, that's terribly good, Jeeves.

JEEVES, *in his consummate skill as a performer, does not allow* BERTIE*'s remarks to break his momentum.*

BASSETT. I never forget a face.

BASSETT *uses his umbrella to swipe the* PROPRIETOR, *who then disappears behind the cabinet.*

You came up before me at my magistrates' court once. But not twice. Good! Learned your lesson, eh? Going straight now? Capital. Now let me see, what was it? Don't tell me. It's coming back. Of course, yes. Bag-snatching.

BERTIE. No, no. It was for pinching a policeman's helmet on Boat Race night.

BASSETT. No, it was for bag-snatching. I remember it distinctly. Still, it's all past and done with now. We have turned over a new leaf, have we not? Splendid. Roderick, come over here.

BERTIE. Roderick?

BASSETT. Roderick Spode.

SPODE. Yes, Sir Watkyn.

BERTIE. I turned and saw a terrifying figure who was six foot eight if he was an inch.

SEPPINGS, *as a monocled* RODERICK SPODE, *complete with Oswald Mosely moustache, has appeared from behind the display case. There is an awkward moment as he steps up onto a platform behind the cabinet in order to appear taller.*

BASSETT. Roderick. I want you to meet this fellow. I gave him three months not long ago for snatching bags at railway stations and it is quite evident that his term in jail has had the most excellent effect on him. He has reformed.

SPODE. Oh, yes? What makes you think he has reformed?

BASSETT. Of course he has reformed. It's perfectly obvious that he is no longer stealing bags. What are you doing now, young man?

SPODE. Stealing umbrellas apparently. I notice he's got yours.

BERTIE *suddenly becomes aware that he is holding* BASSETT*'s umbrella.*

BERTIE. I say. I'm most frightfully sorry. I thought that umbrella was mine.

BERTIE. What had caused me to take up this umbrella, I cannot say, unless it was the primeval instinct which makes a man without an umbrella reach for the nearest one in sight.

BASSETT. That is the trouble with you, young man. You are totally unable to distinguish between *meum* and *tuum*. Well, I am not going to have you arrested this time, but I advise you to be very careful. Come, Roderick.

BASSETT *exits.*

BERTIE. With those two thugs gone...

SPODE *snarls and then disappears behind the display case.*

I heard Aunt Dahlia's voice in my head, saying...

DAHLIA (*voice-over*). Sneer at the cow-creamer.

BERTIE. Thank you, Seppings.

SEPPINGS *comes out to acknowledge* BERTIE.

BERTIE. And I turned to speak to the proprietor.

SEPPINGS, *realising that this should be him, disappears behind the truck and then appears the other side as the* PROPRIETOR.

PROPRIETOR. Can I help?

BERTIE. I understand that you have an eighteenth-century cow-creamer for sale. I wish to sneer… look at it.

The PROPRIETOR *takes out the cow-creamer.*

Oh, tut, tut, tut. Oh dear, dear, dear! Oh, no, no, no, no, no. I don't think much of this. Modern Dutch.

PROPRIETOR. Modern Dutch? It's eighteenth-century English. Look at the 'allmark.

BERTIE. I can't see an 'allmark.

PROPRIETOR. Take it out into the street. It's lighter there.

BERTIE. Right-ho.

BERTIE. I said, and started for the door, when I tripped over a cat…

BERTIE *starts to trip and the explosive sound of a 'meowwwww' can be heard from* JEEVES.

And it was at that very moment that Sir Watkyn Bassett was re-entering the shop. Everything seemed to go into slow motion.

BASSETT *re-enters. Slow-motion sequence in which the cow-creamer flies out of* BERTIE*'s hands and into the air.*

BASSETT. Call a policeman, Roderick!

SPODE. Police!

BASSETT. Police!

BERTIE. Yipped old Bassett up in the tenor clef.

SPODE. Police!

BERTIE. Roared the gorilla, taking the bass. Then the proprietor trilled…

PROPRIETOR. Police!

BERTIE....completing the round, whilst I, contributing nothing, was gone like the wind... (*Jumps into the armchair, miming getting into a cab.*) ...and in the back of a cab within what seemed like seconds.

The doors of the display case are shut and the truck is turned 180 degrees. SEPPINGS *wheels on another section of wall – containing a door, which adjoins the centre section, stage right.*

My original intention was to go to the Drones and get a bite of lunch. But I hadn't gone far when I realised that I wasn't equal to it. I yield to no man in my appreciation of the place... its sparkling conversation, its camaraderie, its atmosphere redolent of all that is brightest in the metropolis... but there would, I knew, be a goodish bit of bread thrown hither and thither at its luncheon table, and I was in no vein to cope with flying bread.

Changing my strategy in a flash, I said to the cabbie, 'Take me to the nearest Turkish bath,' where I had a good steam and was enabled to return to the flat with the roses back in my cheeks.

SEPPINGS *grabs a vaporiser and sprays a cloud of steam from behind* BERTIE*'s head.*

BERTIE. Thank you, cabbie. Keep the... chair.

BERTIE *gets out of the chair and mimes slamming the door. He then exits through the drawing-room door.*

BERTIE. I entered my drawing room.

BERTIE *returns.*

I entered my drawing room.

My fizziness was however turned off at the main by what was awaiting me on the mantelpiece – a telegram from my very good chum, Gussie Fink-Nottle.

GUSSIE (*voice-over*). Come immediately to Totleigh Towers. Serious rift Madeline and self. Unless you come earliest possible moment and lend every effort effect reconciliation, wedding will be broken off.

BERTIE *screws up the telegram and throws it on the floor, but as* GUSSIE*'s voice-over continues, he hurriedly retrieves it from the floor.*

One more thing; am still on speaking terms with Madeline. Expect invitation shortly. Gussie.

JEEVES *appears with a sherry decanter and a glass on a tray.*

JEEVES. Are you ill, sir?

BERTIE. Not ill, Jeeves, but all of a twitter. Read this. But not out loud.

JEEVES *casts his eye over the telegram and then looks back at* BERTIE.

JEEVES. Most disturbing, sir.

BERTIE. Gussie's breaking up with Madeline. What on earth shall I do, Jeeves? You do know what this means?

JEEVES. Perhaps I might explain.

BERTIE. Oh, no. You don't need to explain, Jeeves. I know what's what.

JEEVES. Yes, sir. But there are other parties who may not.

BERTIE. Other parties?

JEEVES *looks out to the audience.*

Oh. Do you know – I was getting so caught up in all of this ghastly business, I completely forgot about them. Yes. You better explain, Jeeves. I can't think straight right now.

JEEVES. When Mr Wooster's very good friend, Mr Fink-Nottle, first endeavoured to formulate a proposal of marriage to Miss Bassett, his courage failed him. On finding himself sitting alone with the young lady after dinner, he admitted to having become the victim of an unfortunate spasm of nervousness and started talking, at some length, about newts. Over the course of several hours he outlined the ways in which British newts differ from Asian newts, and it was when, as midnight approached, he broached the subject of the European newt, that Miss Bassett said she needed to return to her room and dab her temples with eau de Cologne. At which point, as you put it, sir, Mr Fink-Nottle paled over to such a degree that an inexperienced undertaker would have been deceived by his appearance and started embalming him on sight.

BERTIE. Thank you, Jeeves. I think I can take it from here.

BERTIE *addresses the audience.*

BERTIE. So Gussie asked me to do his wooing for him. With the result that Madeline Bassett got it into her head that I was in love with her. She said that she was so sorry to cause me pain, but that her heart belonged to Gussie. Which would have been fine had she not gone on to say that if anything should happen to compel her to give Gussie the heave-ho, I was the next in line. And when a girl comes to you and says that she's returning her betrothed to store and is prepared to sign up with you instead – what can you do except marry her. Well, you have to be civil!

JEEVES. I think under the circumstances, it would be best to proceed to Totleigh Towers and resolve the situation straight away.

BERTIE. Yes, Jeeves. Let's bite the bullet.

BERTIE *pours himself a glass of sherry.*

JEEVES. I will pack immediately.

BERTIE. Oh, and put in that checked suit that I've just had made, will you!

JEEVES. Are you quite sure, sir?

BERTIE. Yes. I need something to cheer me up.

JEEVES. Might I enquire if you are proposing to appear in public in those garments?

BERTIE. Yes, Jeeves. Don't you like them?

JEEVES. A trifle too bizarre, sir, in my opinion.

BERTIE. But lots of fellows have asked who my tailor is.

JEEVES. Doubtless in order to avoid him, sir.

BERTIE. He's supposed to be one of the best men in London.

JEEVES. I am saying nothing about his moral character, sir.

BERTIE. Whatever your opinion, Jeeves, I would still like you to pack it.

JEEVES. Very good, sir...

AUNT DAHLIA *bursts in.*

DAHLIA. Bertie! (*Takes* BERTIE*'s glass and drinks.*) Thank you.

JEEVES. I shall pack immediately.

DAHLIA. Are you off somewhere?

BERTIE. Totleigh Towers.

DAHLIA. Totleigh Towers? Well, I'm dashed! That's just where I came to tell you you had jolly well got to go immediately.

BERTIE. Eh?

DAHLIA. Bertie, you know that devious old guzzler, Sir Watkyn Bassett, your Uncle Tom's biggest rival in the silver-collecting game.

BERTIE. Yes, I've just...

DAHLIA. And you remember that cow-creamer?

BERTIE. Remember it? You will scarcely believe this, Aunt Dahlia, but when I got to the shop, who should be there by the most amazing coincidence but this same Bassett –

DAHLIA. It wasn't a coincidence. He had gone there to have a look at the thing, to see if it was all Tom had said it was. For – can you imagine such lunacy, Bertie? – that chump of an uncle of yours had told the man about it. And now Bassett has bought the cow-creamer for himself, and is taking it down to Totleigh as we speak.

BERTIE. What are you going to do?

DAHLIA. I'm going to pinch the damn thing, of course, or rather you are!

BERTIE. Who, me?

DAHLIA. That's right. See how it all fits in. You're going to stay at Totleigh. You will have a hundred excellent opportunities of getting your hooks on the thing…

BERTIE. But, dash it.

DAHLIA. Perform this simple, easy task for me, or guests at my dinner table will soon be saying: 'Bless my soul what an amazing lunch your chef, Anatole, gave us yesterday! The very pinnacle of haute cuisine. Superb is the only word! I don't wonder you're fond of his cooking. But why is it that we never see Bertie Wooster here any more?'

BERTIE. Aunt Dahlia, this is blackmail!

DAHLIA. Yes, isn't it?

AUNT DAHLIA *allows her parting shot to land and then exits, slamming the door behind her.*

BERTIE. I stared after her and popped a rather suspicious-looking olive into my mouth.

AUNT DAHLIA *scampers across the back of the stage in full view of the audience.*

There was no way out. I had to go to Totleigh.

Lights and music. JEEVES *enters with car coat and goggles for* BERTIE *and then goes to collect a cardboard cut-out of the front of a sports car under his arm, which he sets down on the stage facing the audience.* SEPPINGS *brings two chairs from the wings to represent the driver and passenger seats, and then winds the picture above the fireplace to reveal an image of an avenue of trees.* BERTIE, *meanwhile, does a few Charleston steps.*

The following day, we climbed aboard the two-seater…

They both get in with JEEVES *in the driving seat.* BERTIE *takes the steering wheel off* JEEVES *and they swap seats.* SEPPINGS *meanwhile helps to animate the journey.*

…and bowled along in the direction of Totleigh Towers, self at the wheel, Jeeves at my side. Had circumstances been different, I should no doubt have been feeling at the peak of my form, chatting gaily, waving to passers-by –

SEPPINGS *mimes being a waving passer-by.*

– even singing some light snatch. Unfortunately, however, if there was one thing circumstances weren't, it was different from what they were, and there was no suspicion of a song on my lips.

SEPPINGS *produces his trolley of effects and starts putting them into use.*

BERTIE. Man and boy, Jeeves, I have been in some tough spots in my time, but this one wins the mottled oyster.

JEEVES. Sir?

SEPPINGS *rings a bicycle bell and shakes his fist as a disgruntled cyclist exchanging muttered insults with* BERTIE.

BERTIE. Don't pretend you don't know all about it, Jeeves.

JEEVES. Well, yes, sir, I must confess that I did gather the substance of the conversation. Mrs Travers does have a carrying voice.

BERTIE. Very well, then. You agree with me that the situation is a lulu?

JEEVES. Certainly a sharp crisis in your affairs would appear to have been precipitated, sir.

SEPPINGS *creates bird sounds.* BERTIE *and* JEEVES *look skywards.* BERTIE *loses concentration, so* JEEVES *has to grab the wheel to put him back on course.*

BERTIE. Look at the trouble aunts cause in the world.

SEPPINGS *makes the sound of a cow.*

Are you hungry, Seppings?

Armed with a red disc on a pole, SEPPINGS *acts out the closing of a level crossing and the passing of an express train.*

He's very thorough, isn't he?

JEEVES. Might I venture to enquire if it is your intention to endeavour to carry out Mrs Travers' wishes?

BERTIE. That is the problem that is torturing me, Jeeves. I can't make up my mind. You remember that fellow you've mentioned to me once or twice, who let something wait upon something? You know who I mean – the cat chap.

JEEVES. Macbeth, sir, a character in a play of that name by the late William Shakespeare. He was described as letting 'I dare not' wait upon 'I would', like the poor cat i' th' adage.

SEPPINGS *hold a rain stick up to the microphone.*

BERTIE. Well, that's how it is with me. I wobble, and I vacillate – if that's the word?

JEEVES. Perfectly correct, sir.

SEPPINGS*' effects reach a crescendo with thunder sound effects and rain from a water pistol. He then gets a branch from a tree and lashes it against the car windscreen.*

BERTIE. That's enough, Seppings. Thank you. I think they get the idea.

SEPPINGS *takes the hint and wheels his trolley off.*

It was exceedingly trying meeting Sir Watkyn yesterday and it's going to be a dashed sight more trying if he catches me pinching the cow-creamer.

JEEVES. I quite understand, sir:

> 'And thus the native hue of resolution
> Is sicklied o'er with the pale cast of thought,
> And enterprises of great pitch and moment
> With this regard their currents turn awry
> And lose the name of action.'

BERTIE. Exactly. You take the words out of my mouth.

JEEVES. We're here, sir.

BERTIE. On arriving at Totleigh Towers...

They get out of the car and mime shutting the doors in unison.

...Jeeves took the car round to the stable yard whilst I went in search of the inmates.

While JEEVES *and* SEPPINGS *clear the car and reset the stage,* BERTIE *mime-walks and wanders backwards and forwards across the stage calling out:*

BERTIE. Hello! Hello!... Hello! Hello!...

BERTIE. Old Bassett, I noted, had a magnificent pile here. And I was wondering how long it would have taken him fining, say, twenty people a day five pounds a piece to collect enough to pay for all this.

No, I'm actually asking. How long would it have taken? You first... Oh, hold on, I'll come back to you later.

BERTIE. Hello! Hello!...

Once JEEVES *and* SEPPINGS *have moved the French window into place,* SEPPINGS *finds himself on the inside.* BERTIE *appears outside the French window and mouths 'Hello.'*

JEEVES. Just one moment, sir.

JEEVES *then winds the picture to another image and then nods at* SEPPINGS. *In response,* SEPPINGS *hurriedly dons a wig, transforms himself into* BUTTERFIELD, *the butler, and then opens the door to let* BERTIE *in.*

BERTIE. Sir Watkyn Bassett?

BUTTERFIELD. No, I'm Butterfield the butler, sir.

BERTIE. No, I'm looking for Sir Watkyn Bassett.

BUTTERFIELD. Oh, Mr Wooster, sorry. I fancy he is somewhere in the grounds with Mr Roderick Spode.

BERTIE. Roderick Spode? Big chap with a small moustache and the sort of eye that can open an oyster at sixty paces?

BUTTERFIELD. Yes, sir.

BERTIE. Oh. How about Mr Fink-Nottle?

BUTTERFIELD. I think he has gone for a walk, sir.

BERTIE. Oh? Well, right-ho. Then I'll just potter about in here for a bit.

BUTTERFIELD. Very good, sir.

BERTIE. Thank you, Butterfield.

BUTTERFIELD. No, thank you, sir.

BERTIE. No, thank you.

> BUTTERFIELD *disappears*.

BERTIE. The news that Roderick Spode was on the premises had shaken me a good deal. I mean, imagine how some unfortunate master criminal would feel, on coming down to do a murder at The Old Grange, if he found that not only was Sherlock Holmes putting in the weekend there, but Hercule Poirot, as well. I went in search of a spot of calming tea. Butterfield?

> BERTIE *exits in search of* BUTTERFIELD.

BASSETT. Butterfield?

> BASSETT *strolls into the room, proudly places the cow-creamer on the mantelpiece, kisses it and then leaves*.

> Butterfield?

> BERTIE *reappears*.

BERTIE. Butterfield?

BERTIE. Butterfield? Suddenly, there I was, vis-à-vis, as the expression is, with what could only be described as a silver cow.

> BERTIE *holds the cow-creamer in front of him*.

> Look, it really does 'ave an 'allmark.

> SPODE *has appeared through the French windows*.

SPODE. Hands up!...

BERTIE. No, I was just showing them the 'allmark.

SPODE. Sir Watkyn! Come here, please. I have something to show you.

BERTIE. And, turning, I observed Roderick Spode. He'd grown since our last encounter, being now about nine foot seven.

SPODE, *realising that he's not nearly tall enough, steps up onto a stool*. BASSETT *appears through the door*.

SPODE. Hands up!

BASSETT. Good God! It's the bag-snatcher!

SPODE. Yes. Isn't it incredible?

BASSETT. Well, I'm much obliged to you, Roderick. But what I can't get over is the chap's pertinacity. You would have thought when we foiled that attempt of his in the Brompton Road to steal my umbrella and to raid the antique shop, he would have given up the thing as a bad job. But no. He comes down here the next day to steal my cow-creamer.

SPODE. I suppose this is too serious a case for you to deal with summar... summaril... straight away?

BASSETT. I can issue a warrant for his arrest, Roderick. Bring him along to the library and I'll do it now.

SPODE (*muttering, as he realises that he can't get off the stool*). No, I can't do that.

BERTIE. I was about to explain, after I had secured his attention, that I was on these premises as an invited guest, when Madeline Bassett burst through the French window and said:

JEEVES (*as* BASSETT) *and* SEPPINGS (*as* SPODE) *freeze momentarily, look at each other and realising that one of them has to play the part of* MADELINE BASSETT. JEEVES *spontaneously grabs the shade from a wall lamp and neatly places it on his head. Realising this isn't enough, he unhooks a chiffon curtain from the French window and drapes it around him.* MADELINE *has arrived.*

MADELINE. Goodness gracious! Whatever is all the noise about?... Hello, Bertie.

BERTIE. Jeeves, that's uncanny.

MADELINE. When did you get here?

BERTIE. Oh, hallo. I've just arrived.

MADELINE. Did you have a nice journey down?

BERTIE. Oh, rather, thanks. I came in the two-seater.

MADELINE. You must be quite exhausted.

BERTIE. Oh no, thanks, rather not.

MADELINE. Well, tea will be ready soon. I see you've met Daddy.

The lampshade is removed (as JEEVES *transforms himself back into* BASSETT).

BASSETT. You don't mean you know this man? I've just caught him stealing my cow-creamer.

…and then put back on again.

MADELINE. Daddy, this is my very dear old friend Bertie Wooster. I told you he was coming here today. And naturally your silver would be the first thing he would want to look at. Bertie is Mr Travers' nephew. Your uncle has a wonderful collection, hasn't he, Bertie? I suppose he has often spoken to you of Daddy's.

BERTIE. The whole thing is one of those laughable misunderstandings.

BERTIE *and* MADELINE *look at each other in acknowledgement and break out into a guffaw.* MADELINE *spins round 360 degrees, disposing of curtain and shade as she turns, and coming to rest as a very unconvinced* BASSETT.

As was the episode with the umbrella. You surely must have picked up someone else's umbrella by mistake, before now. The only thing that I've ever pinched was a policeman's helmet and that was on Boat Race night.

BASSETT. That's just as bad as… Sit down, child, sit down.

BASSETT *places* MADELINE's *curtain and shade on the armchair.*

That's just as bad as snatching bags. Isn't it, Roderick?

SPODE. No. I don't think you can go as far as that. When I was at Oxford, I once stole a policeman's helmet myself. A customary prank on high days and holidays.

BASSETT. Well. Even so!

BERTIE *returns the cow-creamer to* BASSETT.

I don't like the smell of this at all. Come, Roderick.

BASSETT *exits.*

SPODE. I've got my eye on you, Wooster.

SEPPINGS *steps down from the stool, which he picks up and carries off with him.*

BERTIE. He said and they biffed off, leaving me alone with…

BERTIE *shuts the door as* MADELINE *reappears from the other side and lounges in the armchair.* BERTIE *turns round to see her.*

…Madeline.

MADELINE. Oh, Bertie, you ought not to be here. Why did you come?… Oh, I know what you're going to say. You felt that cost what it might, you had to see me again, just once. You could not resist the urge to take away with you one last memory, which you could cherish down the lonely years. Oh, Bertie, you remind me of Rudel.

BERTIE. The name was new to me.

BERTIE. Rudel?

MADELINE. The Seigneur Geoffrey Rudel, Prince of Blaye-en-Saintonge.

BERTIE. Never met him, I'm afraid. Pal of yours?

MADELINE. He lived in the Middle Ages. He was a great poet. And he fell in love with the wife of the Lord of Tripoli.

BERTIE. I stirred uneasily. I hoped she was going to keep it clean.

MADELINE. For years he loved her, and at last he could resist no longer. He took the ship to Tripoli and his servants carried him ashore.

BERTIE. Rough crossing, what. Not feeling so good?

MADELINE. He was dying. Of love.

BERTIE. Oh, ah.

MADELINE. They bore him into Lady Melisande's presence on a litter, and he had just strength enough to reach out and touch her hand. Then he died.

BERTIE. She paused and heaved a sigh of relief that seemed to come straight from the camiknickers. A silence ensued.

Long pause.

BERTIE. Teriffic.

BERTIE. I said, feeling I had to say something.

MADELINE *comes over to* BERTIE.

MADELINE. You see now why I said you reminded me of Rudel. Like him you came to take one last look at the woman you loved. But, Bertie, would it not have been cleaner to have ended it all cleanly that day when we said goodbye at Brinkley Court. We had met and you had loved me, and I had to tell you that my heart was another's. That should have been our farewell.

MADELINE *leans too hard against the doorway and accidentally pushes part of the set out of place*.

BERTIE. Absolutely. But, I had a communication from Gussie, more or less indicating that you and he were 'pfft'.

MADELINE. So that's why you came! You thought there might still be some hope? Oh, Bertie, really there is no hope, none. You must not build dream castles in the air. It can only cause you pain. I love Augustus.

BERTIE. Then what did he mean by saying, 'serious rift Madeline and self.'

MADELINE. Oh, that? That was nothing. It was all too silly and ridiculous. Just the teeniest, weeniest little misunderstanding. I thought I found him flirting with my cousin Stephanie, and I was silly and jealous. But he explained everything this morning. He was only taking a fly out of her eye.

BERTIE. So everything's all right between you two now?

MADELINE. Everything. I have never loved Augustus more than I do now. I wonder if you've noticed any difference in him? An improvement, if such a thing were possible. Have you not felt in the past, Bertie, that, if Augustus had a fault, it was a tendency to be a little timid?

BERTIE. Oh, ah, yes, of course, definitely.

BERTIE. I remembered something that Jeeves had once called Gussie.

BERTIE. A sensitive plant, what?

MADELINE. Exactly. You know your Shelley, Bertie.

BERTIE. Oh, am I?

MADELINE. That is what I have always thought him – a sensitive plant. But recently he has shown, together with that wonderful dreamy sweetness of his, a force of character, which I had not suspected he possessed. Why, only this morning, he spoke to Roderick Spode quite sharply. They were arguing about something, and Augustus told him to go and boil his head.

BERTIE. Good Lord!

MADELINE. Sometimes, Bertie, I ask myself if I am worthy of so rare a soul.

BERTIE. Of course you are. You two fit like pork and beans.

MADELINE. It's sweet of you to say so. Many men in your position might have become embittered. But you are too fine for that. Dear Bertie!

MADELINE *gets far too close to* BERTIE.

BERTIE. Thank you, Jeeves.

MADELINE *skips off.*

BERTIE. And on that note we parted, she to go messing about on some domestic errand, I to go in search of a spot of tea.

BUTTERFIELD *appears with a tray.*

BUTTERFIELD. Crumpet, sir.

BERTIE *takes one.*

BERTIE. Thank you, Butterfield.

BUTTERFIELD. No. Thank you, sir.

BERTIE. No, thank you.

GUSSIE FINK-NOTTLE (*played by* JEEVES) *can be heard berating* SPODE *offstage.*

GUSSIE. So kindly do not talk rot, Spode! Do not talk rot! And don't look at me like that.

GUSSIE, *in his thick-lensed, horn-rimmed spectacles, then enters backwards into the room, wagging his finger.*

BERTIE. Ah, Gussie!

GUSSIE. Bertie!

They jump up and down like excited schoolboys.

BERTIE. Gussie!

GUSSIE. Bertie!

BERTIE. Gussie!

GUSSIE. Have a crumpet.

BERTIE. I've already got one.

GUSSIE. Oh yes.

BERTIE. Thank you, Butterfield.

BUTTERFIELD. No. Thank you, sir.

BERTIE. No, thank you.

BUTTERFIELD *withdraws*.

Where's Spode?

GUSSIE. He's gone. With a flea in his ear.

BERTIE. Gussie, what's happened to you? You've changed. I mean, telling Spode not to talk rot. I wouldn't have the nerve to tell Spode not to talk rot.

GUSSIE. Well, to tell you the truth, Bertie, neither would I a week ago.

BERTIE. What happened a week ago?

GUSSIE. A week ago, Bertie, I discovered that I would have to make a speech at the wedding breakfast. The mere idea appalls me. The thought of having to get up in front of hundreds of people with Roderick Spode on one side and Sir Watkyn Bassett on the other…

They break off to check that the coast is clear.

Do you know Sir Watkyn intimately?

BERTIE. Not very. He once fined me five quid for pinching a policeman's helmet on Boat Race night.

GUSSIE. Well, you can take it from me, he's a hard nut and he strongly objects to having me as a son-in-law. For one thing, he would have liked Madeline to marry Spode – who I may mention, has loved her since she was so high. But apart from the fact that she wanted to marry me, Spode didn't want to marry her. He looks upon himself as a Man of Destiny, you see, and feels that marriage would interfere with his mission.

BERTIE. How do you mean, 'his mission'? Is he somebody special?

GUSSIE. Don't you ever read the papers? Roderick Spode is the founder and head of the Saviours of Britain, a fascist organisation better known as the Black Shorts.

BERTIE. Don't you mean 'Shirts'?

GUSSIE. No, by the time Spode formed his association, there were no shirts left.

BERTIE. Golly.

GUSSIE. Yes.

BERTIE. Oh. I saw Madeline just now. She tells me that you are sweethearts still. Correct?

GUSSIE. Quite correct.

GUSSIE *takes his glasses off and talks directly to the standard lamp.*

Oh, Bertie! She's the most beautiful woman I've ever seen. Wouldn't you agree, Bertie?

BERTIE. I'm over here, Gussie.

GUSSIE. There was a little temporary coolness about me taking a fly out of Stephanie Byng's eye, and I got a bit panicked and wired you to come down. However, I took a strong line, and everything is all right now.

BERTIE. But you say Sir Watkyn doesn't approve.

GUSSIE. No, he doesn't approve of anything about me. At our very first meeting I could see that I was not his dream man. And when he learned from Madeline that I was keeping newts in my bedroom...

BERTIE. You're keeping newts in your bedroom here?

GUSSIE. I am in the middle of a very delicate experiment to see if the full moon influences the love life of newts. Anyway, when he heard about my newts, he said something very derogatory – under his breath, but I heard him. So the idea of making a speech in front of him and Spode filled me with a panic and a terror... I didn't see how I was going to face it. And then I thought of Jeeves. I took the train to London and placed my problem before Jeeves, who said that disinclination to speak in public is due to a fear of one's audience.

In perfect sync, BERTIE *and* GUSSIE *turn and stare at the audience.*

BERTIE. Are you afraid of them, Gussie?

GUSSIE. No! We do not, Jeeves said, fear those whom we
despise. The thing to do, therefore, is to cultivate a lofty
contempt for those who will be listening to one. You fill your
mind with scornful thoughts about them. Well, I did better
than that. I wrote them down in a notebook. Have you ever
heard Sir Watkyn Bassett dealing with a bowl of soup...? It's
not unlike the Scottish Express going through a tunnel.

GUSSIE *and* BERTIE *jump up and down with childlike
euphoria.*

Have you ever seen Spode eat asparagus?

BERTIE. No.

GUSSIE. Revolting. It alters one's whole conception of Man as
Nature's last word. But that's nothing. I've written far better
things than that.

BERTIE (*laughing*). If Sir Watkyn or Spode got hold of that
book they'd kill you!

GUSSIE. Yes, they would. (*Laughing.*) And then you'd have to
marry Madeline!

BERTIE (*laughing*). Show me what else you've written.

GUSSIE *reaches into his pocket to consult the book.*

GUSSIE....That's funny. I must have dropped it somewhere.

BERTIE. Dropped it?

GUSSIE *and* BERTIE *frantically search the room.*

GUSSIE. Where is it? Wait a minute. It's beginning to come
back. Yes, I remember. I took it out just before lunch
yesterday to jot down a note when I met Stephanie Byng,
and took the fly out of her eye.

BERTIE. Yes?

GUSSIE. Immediately after I had coped with the fly, I recollect
hearing Stephanie saying, 'Hallo, what's that?' and seeing
her stop and pick something up. It was just at that moment

that I caught sight of Madeline. I think it is obvious that the book is now in the possession of Stephanie Byng.

BERTIE. Stiffy? Where is she now?

GUSSIE. I seem to remember her saying something about walking down to the village with her dog. You might stroll down and meet her.

GUSSIE *exits and then reappears at the side of the stage (without his glasses) as* JEEVES. *He grabs hold of a fly rope and lets down a backdrop of a country house, leaving* BERTIE *alone on stage.*

BERTIE. I had to get that notebook. It did not take me long to get to the end of the drive. At the gates, I paused. It seemed to me that my best plan would be to linger here until Stiffy returned. As I stood musing, a human drama was developing in the road in front of me.

SEPPINGS, *now dressed as* CONSTABLE OATES, *an oversized policeman, rides a bicycle onto the stage.*

A policeman was approaching on a bicycle.

As OATES *rides into the wings, we hear a crash after which* OATES *reappears, followed shortly by a Scottish terrier who starts biting his leg. He grabs hold of the dog and throws it into the wings.* STIFFY BYNG (*played by* JEEVES) *then appears, holding the terrier protectively in her arms.*

STIFFY. Oh. How dare you!

OATES. Miss Byng. This makes twice that the animal has committed an aggravated assault on my bicycle. I shall be forced to register a complaint with Sir Watkyn.

STIFFY. You leave my uncle out of this. And anyway, you shouldn't ride a bicycle. Bartholomew hates bicycles.

Bartholomew barks at appropriate moments.

OATES. I ride a bicycle, miss, because if I didn't I should have to cover my beat on foot.

STIFFY. Do you good. Get some fat off you.

OATES. Ooh. I shall have to summons you once more for being in possession of a savage dorg, not under proper control.

OATES *exits*.

STIFFY. Gosh. Hallo, Bertie. When did you get here?

BERTIE. Oh, recently… Stiffy, passing lightly over all the guff about being charmed to see you again and how well you're looking and all that, have you got a small, brown, leather-covered notebook that Gussie Fink-Nottle dropped yesterday?

STIFFY. Yes. I've got it. I must say it does make splendid reading. Really excellent character studies of Roderick Spode and Uncle Watkyn. Though why anyone should waste their time on those two when there's Oates simply crying out to be written about, I can't imagine. Anyway, I've got a much better way of getting back at Oates. It's something you're rather good at. I'm going to pinch his helmet… or at least Harold is. He's often said he would do anything in the world for me, bless him. We're engaged now, you know.

BERTIE. What. You and the Reverend Harold Pinker?

STIFFY. Yes. But it's frightfully secret. Uncle Watkyn might not approve, particularly at a time when he's reeling at the prospect of having Gussie marrying Madeline. So he mustn't know about Harold until he has been well sweetened. Which is what I wanted to talk to you about. There's something I want you to do for me. It's quite simple. All you have to do is go into Uncle Watkyn's collection room and steal his cow-creamer. It's a sort of cream jug, Bertie.

BERTIE. Yes, I know.

STIFFY. It looks exactly like a cow.

BERTIE. Yes, I know.

STIFFY. But smaller, of course, and made of silver.

BERTIE. Yes, I know.

STIFFY. You'll burst out of the French windows where Harold will be waiting, and you'll hit each other on the nose, then you can escape and he will return the cow-creamer to Uncle Watkyn, in a blaze of glory. Don't you think it's a wonderful scheme, Bertie?

BERTIE. Most. But I'm sorry, I won't do it.

STIFFY. You know, Bertie, I really ought to take that book to Uncle Watkyn. That's what my conscience tells me to do. After all, I owe a lot to him. For years he has been a second father to me. And he ought to know...

BERTIE. Stiffy!

STIFFY. It's no good saying 'Stiffy!' Either you sit and do your bit, or Uncle Watkyn gets some racy light reading over his morning egg and coffee. Think it over, Bertie.

STIFFY *exits*.

BERTIE. I stumbled slowly back towards the house.

BERTIE *walks straight into the backdrop, which is then flown out to reveal the exterior of the French windows at night*.

Just how long it took me, I don't know, but... Oh, I'm here. Winged creatures of the night barged into me, but I gave them little attention. It was not till a voice suddenly spoke several feet above my head that I came out of the coma. It was, of course, Roderick Spode.

SEPPINGS (*as* SPODE) *appears, wheeling on a newly created superstructure of a gigantic, headless body which is mounted onto his stool. He throws open the French windows*.

SPODE. Good evening, Wooster. I should like a word with you.

BERTIE. Oh, yes.

SPODE. I have been talking to Sir Watkyn Bassett and he has told me the whole story of the cow-creamer.

BERTIE. Oh, yes?

SPODE. And we know why you are here.

BERTIE. Oh, yes.

SPODE. Stop saying 'Oh, yes?', you miserable worm, and listen to me. Oh, yes. It is perfectly plain to us why you are here. You have been sent by your Uncle Tom to steal this cow-creamer for him. You needn't trouble to deny it. I found you with the thing in your hands this afternoon. And now, we learn, your Aunt Dahlia is arriving. The muster of the vultures, ha!

BERTIE. What! Is she? Are you sure?

SPODE. Let me warn you, Wooster. If the thing disappears, I shall know where it has gone, and I shall immediately beat you to a jelly. To a jelly. Have you got that clear?

BERTIE. Oh, quite. To a jelly.

SPODE. Splendid.

> SPODE *suddenly becomes aware that* JEEVES *is approaching and abruptly changes his tone.*

> What a lovely evening, is it not? Extraordinarily mild for the time of year. Well, I mustn't keep you any longer. You will be wanting to go and dress for dinner.

> JEEVES *appears.*

JEEVES. Excuse me, sir. Mrs Travers presents her compliments, sir, and desires me to say that she is in the Blue Room and would be glad if you could make it convenient to call upon her there as soon as possible. She has a matter of importance which she wishes to discuss.

SPODE. So Mrs Travers has arrived? His Aunt Dahlia, who's married to his Uncle Tom, the silver collector. I see.

JEEVES. Yes, sir.

SPODE. And has a matter of importance to discuss with Mr Wooster?

JEEVES. Yes, sir.

SPODE. Ha!... Ah! I shall see you at dinner.

> SEPPINGS *breaks off from playing* SPODE *and becomes himself.*

SEPPINGS. Could somebody give me a... No. Never mind!

SEPPINGS (*realising that* JEEVES *is unable to assist*)
struggles out of the contraption and wheels it off himself.

BERTIE. Jeeves, stand by to counsel and advise.

JEEVES. Certainly, sir. But may I ask why?

SEPPINGS *wheels on a gramophone and plays some*
appropriately melodramatic music.

BERTIE. The plot has thickened. I'm being blackmailed by
Stiffy. I'm being blackmailed by Aunt Dahlia. And if I carry
out their demands, I'll be beaten black and blue by Spode. I
might not get out of here alive.

Blackout.

Interval.

ACT TWO

BERTIE *is lying in a bathtub, without any clothes on* (*apparently*). *He looks out at the audience.*

BERTIE. Oh. Hello again.

Content in the knowledge that Jeeves' astute mind would soon unravel the tangled affairs, I took a pre-dinner bath. And after splashing about in the porcelain for a bit, composure began to return. The discovery of a toy duck in the soap dish, presumably the property of some juvenile visitor, contributed not a little to this. For the benefit of those interested, I may mention that if you shove the thing under the surface with a sponge and then let go, it shoots out of the water in a manner calculated to divert the most careworn. (*Demonstrates.*) Ten minutes of this and I was able to get out of the bath, confidently expecting a solution from Jeeves…

BERTIE *starts to get out of the bath.*

…Ah! I haven't really thought this one through. Oh well, back to the duck.

He throws the duck into the air. At that moment, JEEVES *appears with towels and bathrobe. He catches the duck and then holds up a towel in order to preserve* BERTIE*'s modesty as he gets out of the bath.*

JEEVES. Allow me, sir.

BERTIE. Thank you, Jeeves. But unfortunately no solution was forthcoming because Jeeves wasn't there then. Were you, Jeeves?

JEEVES. No, sir.

BERTIE. He's here now, but he wasn't there then. I mean he wasn't there in the story, but he's here now while I'm telling the story. I think that's all fairly straightforward. Isn't it, Jeeves?

JEEVES. Indeed, sir.

BERTIE. To be perfectly frank, I don't normally get out of the bath in front of seven hundred people. Do I, Jeeves?

JEEVES. Not to my knowledge, sir.

BERTIE. I strolled back to my bedroom... Where are you going, Jeeves?

JEEVES. Just one moment, sir.

JEEVES *collects the bicycle, downstage right, attaches it to a drive belt from the floor and starts pedalling. The revolve begins to turn and reveals* BERTIE*'s bedroom. An operational door, positioned on the right-hand side, opens out onto a hallway behind it. A window frame sits side on, stage left, with a single bed in front of it.*

BERTIE. Jeeves, the scenery. It's moving.

JEEVES. Yes, sir.

BERTIE. Are you doing that?

JEEVES. I'm not here, sir.

BERTIE. Am I here?

JEEVES. Oh, yes, sir.

JEEVES *pulls out the screen.*

BERTIE. I'm going to put my socks on. Do you know, I have to say I'm finding this acting business rather easy, I don't know what they make such a fuss about, Jeeves.

JEEVES. I'm still not here, sir.

JEEVES *exits.*

BERTIE....And he wasn't. In his place was...

AUNT DAHLIA *bursts through the door.*

DAHLIA. Bertie!

BERTIE. Oh, golly, old ancestor! Since we last met, there have been new developments and my affairs have become somewhat entangled, I regret to say. You might put it that Hell's foundations are quivering.

DAHLIA. Enough, Bertie. So you're having your troubles too, are you? Well, I don't know what developments there have been your end, but there has been a new development at mine, and it's a stinker. That's why I have come down to Totleigh in such a hurry.

BERTIE. What is it? What's happened?

DAHLIA. Just before I left home this afternoon, a letter arrived for your Uncle Tom from Sir Watkyn Bassett. When I say 'just before I left home', that was what made me leave home. Because do you know what was in it?

BERTIE. What?

DAHLIA. An offer from Sir Watkyn to swap the cow-creamer for Anatole.

BERTIE. Never.

DAHLIA. Yes. Sir Watkyn is now using the cow-creamer to pinch my most treasured possession – my chef!

BERTIE. But surely Uncle Tom would never contemplate giving away the best chef in England for a silver cream jug.

DAHLIA. Wouldn't he? That's all you know. Do you remember Pomeroy, the butler we had before Seppings?

BERTIE. Yes, Seppings... Aunt Dahlia.

DAHLIA. Well, he traded him to the Bessington-Copes for an oviform chocolate pot on three scroll feet.

BERTIE. But Uncle Tom wouldn't do that?

DAHLIA. He certainly would.

AUNT DAHLIA *gets up and walks over to the mantelpiece and surveys the objects on it.* BERTIE *points at a particular piece.*

BERTIE. What about that Infant Samuel at Prayer?

DAHLIA. Thank you... Duck!

AUNT DAHLIA *picks it up and apparently hurls it against the opposite wall. Sound effect of china smashing, but* AUNT DAHLIA *does a double take, revealing that the ornament is still in her hand. She surreptitiously puts it back on the mantelpiece.*

I tell you, Bertie, there are no lengths to which a really loony collector will not go to to secure a coveted specimen. The only thing that stopped your Uncle Tom wiring Sir Watkyn there and then that it was a deal was my telling him that you had gone to Totleigh Towers expressly to pinch the cow-creamer, and that he would have it in his hands almost immediately. So I hope you've got all your plans cut and dried. We can't afford to waste time. Every moment is precious…

AUNT DAHLIA *exits, slamming the door behind her. The door opens again, almost immediately, and* JEEVES *enters.*

BERTIE. Jeeves. Where have you been?

JEEVES. I beg your pardon, sir. I have just been in conversation with Mr Fink-Nottle.

BERTIE. Oh well, never mind about him. I've just been in conversation with Mrs Travers. We all have conversations, Jeeves.

BERTIE *goes behind the screen and starts to dress for dinner.*

And as you might say – a sharp crisis in my affairs has indeed been precipitated. Have you come up with anything yet, Jeeves?

JEEVES. Not yet, sir, I regret to say.

BERTIE. What. No results whatever?

JEEVES. No, sir. I regret to say.

BERTIE (*popping his head up from behind the screen*). I lied. There are two boring bits.

BERTIE *comes out from behind the screen and continues to dress, assisted by* JEEVES.

It may be, Jeeves, that you and the audience haven't got the whole scenario clear in your minds. Item one – Aunt Dahlia says that if I don't pinch the cow-creamer and hand it over to her, not only will she bar me from her table, and deprive me of Anatole's cooking, but she is also in danger of losing the man altogether.

JEEVES. Yes, sir.

BERTIE. Item two – if I do pinch the cow-creamer and hand it over to her, Spode will beat me to a jelly.

JEEVES. Yes, sir.

BERTIE. Item three – if I pinch it and hand it over to her and don't pinch it and hand it over to Harold Pinker, not only shall I undergo the jellying process alluded to above, but Stiffy will take that notebook of Gussie's and hand it over to Sir Watkyn Bassett. And you know what the result of that would be...

JEEVES. Yes, sir. You would be expected to marry Miss Bassett.

BERTIE. Yes, I know... Well, there you are. That's the set-up.

JEEVES. Yes, sir. It is certainly a somewhat unfortunate state of affairs.

BERTIE. Jeeves, don't try me too high. Not at a moment like this.

JEEVES. Indeed, sir.

Yes, sir. The trousers perhaps a quarter of an inch higher, sir. One aims at the carelessly graceful break over the instep. It is a matter of the nicest adjustment.

BERTIE *hitches up the waistband of his trousers very slightly.*

BERTIE. Like that?

JEEVES. Admirable, sir.

BERTIE. There are moments, Jeeves, when one asks oneself 'Do trousers matter?'

JEEVES. The mood will pass.

BERTIE. I don't see why it should. If you can't think of a way out of this mess, it seems to me that it is the end... You know, I've been wondering if this man Spode hasn't some shady secret. Do you know anything about him, Jeeves?

JEEVES. No, sir. Still, it might be worthwhile to institute enquiries.

BERTIE. Yes, but where?

JEEVES. I was thinking of the Junior Ganymede, sir. It is a club for gentlemen's personal gentlemen in Curzon Street, to which I have belonged for some years. The personal attendant of a gentleman of Mr Spode's prominence would be sure to be a member, and he would, of course, have confided to the secretary a good deal of material concerning him for insertion in the club book.

BERTIE. Eh?

JEEVES. Under Rule Eleven, every new member is required to supply the club with full information regarding his employer. This not only provides entertaining reading, but also serves as a warning to members who may be contemplating taking service with gentlemen who fall short of the ideal.

BERTIE. A thought struck me, and I started. Indeed, I started rather violently.

BERTIE. What happened when you joined?

JEEVES. Sir?

BERTIE. Did you tell them all about me?

JEEVES. Oh, yes, sir.

BERTIE. What, everything? The time when I came home after Pongo Twistleton's birthday party and mistook the standard lamp for a burglar?

JEEVES. Yes, sir. That episode is a particular favourite with members, sir. They like to have these things to read on wet afternoons.

BERTIE. Oh, they do, do they? And suppose some wet afternoon it falls into the wrong pair of hands.

JEEVES. The contingency of 'the wrong pair of hands', as you call them, obtaining access to the club book is a remote one. It is only available to members.

BERTIE. I dare say. But recent events under this roof will have shown you how the wrong pair of hands can obtain access to books... Anyway, what's your idea? To apply to the secretary of your club for information about Spode?

JEEVES. Yes, sir.

BERTIE. You think he'll give it to you?

JEEVES. Oh, yes, sir.

BERTIE. How soon could you get in touch with him?

JEEVES. I could ring him on the telephone immediately, sir.

BERTIE. Then do so, Jeeves. I could yet avoid the jellyfication process.

JEEVES. Yes, sir... I beg your pardon, sir. I have been in conversation with Mr Fink-Nottle, sir.

BERTIE. And has Gussie anything new to report?

JEEVES. Yes, sir. It appears that his relations with Miss Bassett have been severed. The engagement is broken off.

JEEVES *exits.* BERTIE *looks blankly at the audience.*

BERTIE. The news hit me like one who, picking daisies on the railway, catches the 4.15 in the small of the back.

A spotlight comes up on BERTIE *who has positioned himself downstage centre to talk to the audience.*

I went down to dinner but the sight of Gussie and Madeline sitting side by side at the other end of the table turned the food to ashes in my mouth. There could be no question whatever that Jeeves was right. As far as I was able to ascertain, they didn't exchange a word from start to finish. Oh, yes, once, when he asked her to pass the salt and she passed the pepper, and he said, 'I meant the salt,' and she said, 'Oh, really?' and passed the mustard. At which point Gussie got up and left the table. Sir Watkyn and Spode glowered after him and while they were glowering, I murmured something about fetching my cigarette case, sidled out, returned to my room and lit a thoughtful gasper…

There are three knocks on the door. JEEVES *then opens it and assists* SPODE *in bringing the Spodemobile into the room.*

SPODE. Ah, Wooster! I thought Fink-Nottle might be here.

BERTIE. Well, he isn't. Any message I can give him if he shows up?

SPODE. Yes. You can tell him that I'm going to break his neck.

BERTIE. Break his neck. I see. Right-ho. And if he asks why?

SPODE. He knows why. Because he is a butterfly who toys with women's hearts and throws them away like soiled gloves.

SPODE *mimes this, disdainfully.*

BERTIE. Right-ho. I hadn't had a notion that that was what butterflies did.

SPODE. Well, they do.

BERTIE. Most interesting. Well, I'll let him know if I run across him.

SPODE. To a jelly, Wooster. To a jelly…

SPODE *realises that he is unable to back out of the door.*

Aren't you going to show me out?

BERTIE. Eh?

SPODE. I need a push.

BERTIE. Oh, yes!

BERTIE *assists* SPODE *with backing the Spodemobile out of the room and then shuts the door. At that moment,* GUSSIE *sticks his head out from underneath the bed.*

GUSSIE. Bertie, I say! That was a close call. (*Crawls out and rushes over to the door.*) I think I'll lock the door, if you don't mind. He might come back. Why he didn't look under the bed, I can't imagine. (*Starts talking to the standard lamp.*) I always thought these dictators were so thorough.

BERTIE. Gussie, I'm over here. Never mind about beds and dictators. What's all this about you and Madeline Bassett? What on earth has she broken off the engagement for? What did you do to her?

GUSSIE. It wasn't so much what I did to her – it was what I did to Stephanie Byng. After you had spoken to her in the garden, she informed me that she was not prepared to release the notebook. So I decided that I would retrieve it by some other means. I had a theory that she would be carrying it on her person, in some private place like her stocking, to keep it safe and had the idea of involving her in some sort of friendly romp, during which I could snatch the book from her.

Anyway, I heard her singing folk songs in the drawing room. I went down there, and there she was at the piano, all alone... At least, I thought she was all alone... What I didn't know, you see, was that Madeline, though invisible for the moment, was also in the room. She had gone behind a screen to get a further supply of folk songs... and... well, the long and the short of it is, just as I was testing out my theory and romping... and checking Stiffy's stockings, out came Madeline... and... Well, it was not easy to pass it off. As a matter of fact, I didn't pass it off. That's the whole story. Bertie, how are you on knotting sheets?

BERTIE. Knotting sheets?

GUSSIE. Yes. I was thinking it over under the bed, while you and Spode were chatting, and I came to the conclusion that the only thing to be done is for us to take the sheets off your bed...

GUSSIE *takes a sheet off the bed.*

...like I've just done, and tie knots in them, and then you can lower me down from the window.

GUSSIE *climbs up onto the windowsill and opens the window.*

They do it in books, and I have an idea I've seen it in the movies. Once outside, I can take your car and drive up to London. After that my plans are uncertain. I may go to California.

BERTIE. California?

Noises off.

GUSSIE. He's coming.

BERTIE *goes to the door and* GUSSIE *hides back underneath the bed.* BERTIE *then turns back to find that* GUSSIE *has disappeared. He looks out of the window in horror.*

BERTIE. Gussie?... Gussie?... Gussie?

GUSSIE (*voice-over*). I'm down here.

BERTIE. Oh, right. Sorry.

BERTIE *crouches down and continues to plead with him.*

There you are... But, Gussie, pull yourself together. You can't just run away to California.

GUSSIE (*voice-over*). It's seven thousand miles away. Spode would hardly go to California.

BERTIE. What you've got to do is get that notebook. If you secured that book and showed it to Madeline, its contents would convince her that your motives in acting as you did towards Stiffy were not what she suspected...

BERTIE *turns around as* JEEVES *appears through the door.*

...Ah, Jeeves. No time to explain but Gussie's under the bed. Did you connect with the secretary of your club?

JEEVES. Yes, sir. I have just finished speaking to him.

BERTIE. Tell me all.

JEEVES. I fear I cannot do that, sir. The rules of the club regarding the dissemination of material recorded in the book are rigid.

However, if we may have a private word, sir.

JEEVES *goes to a place out of earshot.* BERTIE *lifts up the bedspread and reassures* GUSSIE *before going over to join* JEEVES.

BERTIE. Just one moment, Gussie.

JEEVES. It is only the details of the matter which I am precluded from mentioning. I am perfectly at liberty to tell you that it would greatly lessen Mr Spode's potentiality for evil, if you were to inform him that you know all about Eulalie, sir.

BERTIE. Eulalie.

JEEVES. Eulalie, sir.

BERTIE. Eulalie.

JEEVES. Eulalie.

BERTIE. You're sure you can't go a bit deeper into the subject?

JEEVES. Quite sure, sir. Were I to do so, it is probable that my resignation from the club would be called for.

BERTIE. Just saying 'Eulalie' would really put a stopper on him?

JEEVES. Yes, sir.

BERTIE. Oh well. Thank you, Jeeves, that will be all.

JEEVES. Thank you, sir.

JEEVES *retires and* BERTIE *gets into his stride.*

BERTIE. It's all right, Gussie, we have nothing to fear. I have just learned something about Spode, which he wouldn't care to have generally known… Ah. Someone approaches. This may be the blighter now.

GUSSIE *calls out from underneath the bed.*

GUSSIE (*voice-over*). Lock that door!

BERTIE. It will not be necessary.

GUSSIE (*voice-over*). Lock the door!

BERTIE. Let him come. I positively welcome this visit.

GUSSIE. Please lock that door.

BERTIE. Watch me deal with him, Gussie. It will amuse you.

GUSSIE *appears from underneath the bed in an attempt to lock the door. He is however too late.* SPODE *has made his entrance.*

SPODE. Ah, Fink-Nottle. I knew you were here.

BERTIE. Well, Spode, what is it now?

SPODE. Get out of my way, Wooster...

BERTIE *runs round to get in front of him.*

BERTIE. No!

SPODE. Ha. Well, what do you want?

BERTIE. What do I want? I like that. That's good. Since you ask, Spode, I want to know what the devil you mean by coming into my private apartment, taking up space, which I require for other purposes and interrupting me when I am chatting with my personal friends. Really, one gets about as much privacy in this house as a striptease dancer. I assume that you have a room of your own. Get back to it, you overgrown slob, and stay there.

SPODE. I will attend to you later, Wooster.

BERTIE. And I will attend to you now, Spode. Gussie, you can come out now.

GUSSIE. Are you quite sure about that, Bertie?

BERTIE. I can guarantee you will no longer be troubled by this gorilla.

SPODE (*sounding like a gorilla*). Who? Who? Who? Who?

GUSSIE *comes out.*

BERTIE. Spode, I know your secret.

BERTIE *takes out a cigarette and lights it.*

…I know all about…

SPODE. All about what?

BERTIE. It was to ask myself the same question that I paused. For, believe me or believe me not, the name which Jeeves had mentioned to me had completely passed from my mind.

SPODE. All about what?

BERTIE. Well, as a matter of fact, I've forgotten.

GUSSIE *whimpers*.

I'm sorry.

SPODE. I'm going to break your neck, Fink-Nottle, just as soon as I can get over to you.

BERTIE. Oh, right.

BERTIE *pushes the Spodemobile towards* GUSSIE.

BERTIE. As Spode advanced menacingly towards Gussie, I was able to spring into action.

BERTIE *tears an oil painting off the wall and smashes it over* SPODE*'s head*.

I switched off the lights…

JEEVES *takes his* GUSSIE *glasses off for a second and clicks his fingers. Semi-blackout.*

…Gussie threw me the sheet from the bed and, I… (*Spends, what feels like, an eternity trying to unfold the sheet.*) with the swiftness of a tiger, pounced upon Spode – enveloping him completely.

BERTIE *finally throws the sheet over the top of the Spodemobile.* GUSSIE *rushes out of the door.*

Following the sound caused by Gussie exiting, Spode pursued him into the hallway, where he collided with a solid *object and fell back into the room.*

A dummy of SPODE *is thrown back into the room.* BERTIE *checks to see if he is 'still with us'.*

BERTIE. Spode! Spode! I think he's seriously hurt!

BERTIE runs in and out of the room. AUNT DAHLIA enters and switches on the lights. BERTIE manipulates the dummy to keep it 'alive'.

DAHLIA. Bertie, Bertie… What is this joint? A loony bin? Who the devil's that inside the – sheet?

BERTIE. It's Spode. But he's out cold.

DAHLIA. Spode? Then why don't you help me get him up. I don't believe we've met.

BERTIE. I made the introductions.

BERTIE assists the sheeted dummy up to a standing position.

BERTIE. Mr Roderick Spode, Mrs Travers.

DAHLIA. Charmed. What on earth have you got that sheet around you for? Wear it if you like, of course. But it doesn't suit you.

AUNT DAHLIA pulls a compact from her pocket and turns away from the audience to powder her nose in order to produce SPODE's voice.

SPODE. I must ask you to leave us, madam. I am going to thrash this man within an inch of his life.

DAHLIA. You don't touch a nephew of mine.

SPODE. I am going to break every bone in his body.

DAHLIA. You aren't doing anything of the sort. The idea!

SPODE and AUNT DAHLIA confront each other at the door and gradually exit.

I have dealt with far bigger men than you, Mr Spode.

SPODE. Mrs Travers. I need to speak to you in private.

DAHLIA. Your tone is unnecessarily threatening.

The head of the SPODE dummy hits the top of the doorframe as AUNT DAHLIA pushes him out.

SPODE. Ow!

DAHLIA. Sorry!

SPODE. Mrs Travers, I would never touch a woman and I'm asking you not to touch a man. Please unhand me.

DAHLIA. Only if you promise to be civil.

SPODE. As a gentleman, I give you my word.

DAHLIA. Very well then, I'm sorry.

SPODE seizes his moment and returns to the room on the Spodemobile.

SPODE. Your gullible aunt can't help you now…

SPODE shuts the door. We hear knocking and he puts a hand in front of his mouth to disguise the fact that he is producing AUNT DAHLIA*'s voice.*

DAHLIA. Bertie, Bertie. He's locked the door.

SPODE. Please, Mrs Travers… You…

BERTIE. You…

SPODE. You…

BERTIE. You…

SPODE. You!

BERTIE. Eulalie! That's it, Spode. I know all about Eulalie.

SPODE. Oh, do you?

BERTIE. I do.

The door handle is rattled and we hear AUNT DAHLIA*'s voice again.*

DAHLIA. Bertie, Bertie!

BERTIE. It's all right, Aunt Dahlia. Everything's under control.

SPODE. Er – how did you find out?

BERTIE. I have my methods.

SPODE. Oh? I hope you will keep this to yourself, Wooster? You will keep it to yourself, won't you, Wooster?

BERTIE. I will...

SPODE. Thank you, Wooster.

BERTIE. ...provided that we have no more of these extraordinary exhibitions on your part of – what's the word? Imperviousness? No, it's not imperviousness. Imposition? No it's not imposition. It's on the tip of my tongue. Begins with an 'i' and means being a jolly sight too impolite. But it's not impolite.

The top of a ladder appears from the other side of the window and JEEVES*'s head suddenly pops into view.*

JEEVES. Impertinence, sir.

BERTIE. That's it. Impertinence, Spode.

SPODE. Of course, of course. I'm afraid I have been acting rather hastily. Did I rumple your coat, Wooster? I'm sorry. I forgot myself. It shall not happen again. I'm sorry I called you a miserable worm, Wooster. I spoke without thinking.

BERTIE. Always think, Spode. Well, that is all. You may withdraw.

SPODE. Thank you, Wooster. I shall trouble you no further. Goodnight, Wooster.

BERTIE. Goodnight, Spode.

SPODE. I need a push.

BERTIE. Oh, yes.

SPODE *backs out through the doorway.*

SPODE. Goodnight, Wooster.

BERTIE. Goodnight, Spode.

SPODE. Goodnight, Mrs Travers. Thank you again for being so understanding.

DAHLIA. Well, that's quite all right. Goodnight, Mr Spode.

AUNT DAHLIA *reappears at the doorway.*

Don't worry, Bertie. (*Realising that she is not wearing her hat/wig, she exits to fetch it and re-enters properly attired.*) Don't worry, Bertie. I heard it all. Good old blackmail! You can't beat it. I've always said so and always shall. Do you realise what this means? Now that you've got the goods on Spode, the main obstacle to your stealing the cow-creamer has been removed.

BERTIE. I'm afraid, Aunt Dahlia, that life is not as straightforward as that. Spode may have ceased to be a danger to the traffic, but that doesn't alter the fact that Stiffy has the notebook. Before taking any steps in the direction of the cow-creamer, I have got to get that notebook and turn it over to Gussie so that he can prove his innocence to Madeline regarding the whole Stiffy stocking scandal…

DAHLIA. Well, that's not my problem. I need that cow-creamer – NOW!

She looks at him disapprovingly and then exits. STIFFY *appears immediately afterwards, gleefully waving a policeman's helmet in front of her.*

STIFFY. Bertie. Look what Harold's just brought me. Constable Oates' helmet. Isn't it just so funny.

BERTIE. Oh, jolly good. Well, seeing as you're in such a good mood, Stiffy, perhaps you would now hand over to me that notebook.

STIFFY. Not until you've done your little task. Steal the cow-creamer, give it to Harold and then let him hit you in the face. Or I'll tell Constable Oates you stole his helmet.

BERTIE. But, Stiffy, old girl, be reasonable. Use the bean.

STIFFY. Not until you've done your little task, Bertie.

STIFFY *exits, leaving the door open. Bartholomew on a lead appears, pulling* BUTTERFIELD *into the room.*

BERTIE. The next moment I found myself gazing into the eyes of the dog Bartholomew, which were fixed on me with the

sinister intentness which is characteristic of this breed of
animal, viz. Aberdeen Terriers.

BUTTERFIELD. I'm sorry, sir. He must have heard Miss
Byng's voice. I'll take him out immediately, sir.

BERTIE *jumps up onto the mantelpiece.*

BERTIE. Thank you, Butterfield.

BUTTERFIELD. No. Thank you, sir.

BERTIE. No, thank you. Butterfield.

Bartholomew chases BERTIE *and jumps up onto the bed.*

What are you doing with that animal?

BUTTERFIELD. I've been charged by Sir Watkyn to lock up
Bartholomew in a kennel.

BERTIE. Good. Why?

BUTTERFIELD. He has requested Constable Oates to guard
his silver collection. I think he has in mind a sort of military
cordon. But the officer won't come anywhere near Totleigh
Towers unless the animal is heavily sedated.

Bartholomew starts to bark.

Down, boy. Leave it!

Bartholomew is not restrained.

BERTIE. You can't talk to an Aberdeen Terrier like that,
Butterfield. Except perhaps for Dobermann Pinschers, there
is no breed of dog quicker to take offence.

JEEVES *enters and glares at Bartholomew, who cowers and
rolls over.*

JEEVES. Good evening, sir. Thank you, Butterfield.

BUTTERFIELD. No, thank you, Jeeves.

BUTTERFIELD *exits.*

BERTIE. A hearty vote of thanks, Jeeves. You said Eulalie
would make Spode wilt and it did. But, we have yet to

straddle the real Becher's Brook, that young Stiffy continues in possession of the notebook, which she will not give me until I have performed her little task and said task is about to get much harder.

JEEVES. Sir?

BERTIE. Sir Watkyn intends to employ Constable Oates to throw a sort of military cordon around his silver collection... This entire scheme will end in disaster... Wouldn't you agree, Jeeves?

JEEVES. Yes, sir. It undoubtedly presents certain grave difficulties. I wonder if I might be permitted to suggest an alternative scheme. The idea I have in mind is to endeavour to take advantage of Sir Watkyn Bassett's attitude towards yourself.

BERTIE. Eh?

JEEVES. He does not like you, sir.

BERTIE. Well, I don't like him.

JEEVES. No, sir. But the important thing is that he has conceived a strong distaste for you, and would consequently sustain a severe shock, were you to inform him that you and Miss Byng were betrothed and were anxious to unite in matrimony.

BERTIE. You want me to marry Stiffy Byng?

JEEVES. No, sir. Merely to ask Sir Watkyn for her hand.

BERTIE. It sounds goofy to me. Where would that get us, Jeeves?

JEEVES. If I might explain, sir.

BERTIE. Yes. Please do.

JEEVES. Sir Watkyn's reactions would be of a strongly defined character.

BERTIE. I'll say! He would hit the ceiling.

JEEVES. Exactly, sir. A very colourful piece of imagery. And if Miss Byng were then to assure him that there was no truth in your statement that you were going to marry her, adding that she was, in fact, betrothed to Mr Pinker, I think the overwhelming relief which he would feel at the prospect that you were not to be part of the family, would lead Sir Watkyn to look with a kindly eye on her union with Mr Pinker.

BERTIE. Oh! You really think that I should do this, Jeeves?

JEEVES. I think it would prove effective, sir.

BERTIE. Where is this frightful uncle of hers?

JEEVES. I suspect that he may be in the library now. I will apprise Ms Byng of our plan.

BERTIE. If you can find her.

JEEVES. It will, I am certain, meet with her approval.

   JEEVES *exits*.

BERTIE. Very well, Jeeves.

BERTIE. So I screwed my courage to the sticking plaster... I was ready to face Sir Watkyn.

   There is a knock at the door. BERTIE *opens it.*

OATES. Excuse me, Mr Wooster. I have reason to believe that my helmet is in this room.

BERTIE. In this room? There must be some mistake.

OATES. Then you won't mind if I undertake a search.

BERTIE. *Avec plaisir*.

   He begins to look around the room. When OATES *is looking under the bed,* BERTIE *tosses* OATES' *helmet into the front row of the audience.*

BERTIE. Here, hold this!

OATES. Everything appears to be in order for the moment.

   OATES *comes out from underneath the bed with one of his whiskers stuck to his forehead.*

BERTIE. Seppings. It's you!

SEPPINGS. Oh, my whiskers… I should have got a stronger glue.

BERTIE. Jeeves was right. You do have a 'particular aptitude for impersonations'.

SEPPINGS. I'm still not in a position to judge, sir… Excuse me, sir. I have another little job to perform.

SEPPINGS goes over to the bike, climbs onto it and starts pedalling. The set starts to revolve, leaving BERTIE *disorientated.*

BERTIE. Jeeves, the scenery's moving again.

BERTIE pops his head round the side of the set as the revolve comes to a standstill – revealing the library, where BASSETT (*played by* JEEVES) *is seated listening to someone on the other end of the telephone.*

Where's the door?

Using the telephone receiver, BASSETT *points him in the right direction.*

…Thank you.

As BERTIE *appears in the doorway,* BASSETT *breaks off from his conversation.*

Sir Watkyn.

BASSETT. Excuse me one moment… Yes, Mr Wooster?

BERTIE. Oh – ah – could I speak to you for a moment?

BASSETT. Speak to me? Why, yes… That is… If you really… Oh, certainly… Pray take a seat.

BERTIE takes up his invitation. BASSETT *returns to his telephone conversation.*

Yes. Butterfield has dealt with the dog. Constable Oates can make his way over now… What do you mean?… Oh, he's here already… Well, I shall look out for him.

He replaces the receiver and then looks over at BERTIE.

That was Totleigh-in-the-Wold Police Station, Mr Wooster.

BERTIE. Oh yes?

BASSETT. Yes. Somebody stole Constable Oates' helmet tonight.

BERTIE. Oh, yes?

BASSETT. Yes, and I intend to find out who the culprit is.

BERTIE. Oh yes?

BASSETT. Yes.

BERTIE. Yes. Rather funny, I mean to say, a chap who's supposed to stop chaps from pinching things from chaps having a chap come along and pinch something from that chap.

BASSETT. Well, Mr Wooster, I think you were about to tell me what brings you here?

BERTIE. Oh, ah, yes. Thanks for reminding me. Have you ever thought about love?

BASSETT. I beg your pardon?

BERTIE. About love. Have you ever brooded on it to any extent?

BASSETT. You have not come here to discuss love.

BERTIE. Yes, I have. That's exactly it. I wonder if you have noticed a rather rummy thing about it – viz., that it is everywhere. You can't get away from it. Love, I mean. Wherever you go, there it is, buzzing along in every class of life. Quite remarkable. Take newts, for instance... Newts.

BERTIE *does a newt impression.*

BASSETT. I am afraid, Mr Wooster, that you will think me quite dense, but I have not the remotest notion what you are talking about.

BERTIE. I'm talking about me and Stiffy.

BASSETT. Stephanie? My niece?

BERTIE. That's right. Your niece. Sir Watkyn, I have the honour to ask you for your niece's hand.

BASSETT. I don't understand.

BERTIE. It's quite simple. I want to marry young Stiffy. She wants to marry me.

BASSETT. She wants to marry you?

BERTIE. You will not be losing a niece. You will be gaining a nephew.

BASSETT. But I don't want a nephew, damn it!

BASSETT *rises from his chair, calling out as he does so.*

Butterfield.

BUTTERFIELD *appears.*

BUTTERFIELD. Sir?

BASSETT. Find Miss Stephanie and tell her that I wish to speak to her.

BUTTERFIELD. Sir!

BASSET *pauses as he has a moment of realisation.*

BASSETT. Oh, never mind. I'll do it myself... Stephanie.

BASSETT *exits and then returns, dressed in a half-and-half costume as* STIFFY *on one side and* BASSETT *on the other.*

STIFFY. You want to see me, Uncle Watkyn?

STIFFY *turns 180 degrees to reveal the* BASSETT *profile.*

BASSETT. Yes, I want to have a word with you. Take my hand. Walk by my side. Sit down. Sit down.

BASSETT *swivels round to become* STIFFY. *The switching of position continues to happen as the dialogue unfolds.*

STIFFY. Oh, hallo, Bertie. I didn't know you were here. Have you and Uncle Watkyn been having a nice talk?

BASSETT. 'Nice' is not the adjective I would have selected.

STIFFY. Oh?

BASSETT. Mr Wooster has just informed me that he wishes to marry you.

STIFFY. Oh, Bertie, I'm terribly flattered and grateful... And, well, all that sort of thing. But, Bertie dear, I'm terribly sorry. I'm afraid it's impossible. I'm in love with someone else.

BASSETT. Eh, who?

STIFFY. Harold Pinker. We've been secretly engaged for weeks.

BASSETT. The whole thing is quite absurd and utterly out of the question. I refuse to consider the idea for an instant.

STIFFY. But what have you got against Harold?

BASSETT. What means has he, if any, beyond his stipend?

STIFFY. About five hundred a year. But what does money matter?

BASSETT. It matters a great deal.

STIFFY. You really feel that, do you?

BASSETT. Certainly. You must be practical.

STIFFY. Right-ho, I will. If you'd rather I married for money, I'll marry for money. Bertie, it's on. Start getting measured for the wedding trousers.

BASSETT. No, not Wooster. Anyone but Wooster. My dear child, don't talk such nonsense. You are quite mistaken. You must have completely misunderstood me. Please sit again. I have no prejudice against this young man Pinker.

STIFFY. No?

BASSETT. I like and respect him.

STIFFY. Oh?

BASSETT. If you really think your happiness lies in becoming his wife –

STIFFY. Um. I do.

BASSETT. I would be the last man to stand in your way.

STIFFY. Thank you, Uncle Watkyn. I will go and tell Harold the good news.

BASSETT. By all means, marry Harold Pinker. The alternative would make me uncle to a newt-impersonating lunatic.

BASSETT *stares at* BERTIE *and then goes out, slamming the door behind him.*

BERTIE. Well, apart from having to do a newt impression, I think that went tremendously well.

BUTTERFIELD *coughs.*

BERTIE. Yes, Butterfield.

BUTTERFIELD. Excuse me, sir, but on her way out, Miss Byng gave me this notebook to give to you, sir.

BERTIE. Oh, thank you, Butterfield.

BUTTERFIELD. No, thank you, sir.

BERTIE. Have you seen Mr Fink-Nottle?

BUTTERFIELD. Yes, sir, he is in the drawing room with Miss Bassett.

BERTIE. That couldn't be more perfect. Would you be so kind as to present this to him.

BUTTERFIELD. Certainly, sir.

BERTIE. Thank you, Butterfield.

BUTTERFIELD. No, thank you, sir.

BUTTERFIELD *turns back into* SEPPINGS *and goes over to the bicycle and starts pedalling in order to operate the revolve.* JEEVES *then enters* BERTIE*'s room, which appears to be empty.*

JEEVES. Sir?

BERTIE *enters the room through the window.*

BERTIE. I'm sorry. I can't work out the scenery. Where did the door go? By the way, I meant to say, Jeeves – this bears more than a passing resemblance to my room at Totleigh. The only thing that's missing…

JEEVES. Just one moment, sir.

JEEVES *walks over to the fly ropes and lowers a section of ceiling onto the set.* BERTIE *looks on aghast.*

BERTIE. Jeeves, you never cease to amaze.

JEEVES. Thank you, sir.

BERTIE. Well, that plan of yours worked all right, Jeeves. An uncle's blessing came popping out like a cork out of a champagne bottle. Spode is neutered. Gussie's in the clear. The only remaining fly in the remaining ointment is that Aunt Dahlia hasn't got the cow-creamer.

JEEVES. Yes, sir. Regarding that little matter, I was detained by Constable Oates. It would appear that the officer had met with an accident. He was assaulted while endeavouring to recover Sir Watkyn's cow-creamer from a midnight marauder, sir.

BERTIE. Somebody pinched the cow-creamer? But I was supposed to do that. What happened, Jeeves?

JEEVES. Well, sir, I gather that, alerted by the sound of breaking glass, the constable entered the collection room just in time to catch sight of a dim figure stealing out through the French window. He pursued it into the garden, and was overtaking it and might shortly have succeeded in effecting an arrest, when there sprang from the darkness a dim figure –

BERTIE. The same dim figure?

JEEVES. No, sir. Another one.

BERTIE. A big night for dim figures.

JEEVES. Yes, sir.

BERTIE. Is Constable Oates a dim figure?

JEEVES. Not in this context. No, sir.

BERTIE. Better call these dim figures Pat and Mike, or we shall be getting mixed.

JEEVES. A and B perhaps, sir?

BERTIE. If you prefer it, Jeeves. So Oates had just caught up with dim figure A, you say, when dim figure B sprang from the darkness –

JEEVES. – and struck Constable Oates upon the nose.

BERTIE. Harold Pinker! He was supposed to punch me.

JEEVES. Yes, sir. No doubt Miss Byng inadvertently forgot to apprise him that there had been a change in the evening's arrangements.

BERTIE. What became of Harold?

JEEVES. On becoming aware of the officer's identity, he apologised, sir, and then withdrew.

BERTIE. Well, I don't know what to make of this, Jeeves. This dim figure. I am referring to dim figure A. Who could it have been? Had Oates any views on the subject?

JEEVES. Very definite views, sir. He is convinced that it was you.

BERTIE. Me, Jeeves?

JEEVES. And it is his intention, as soon as he is able to secure Sir Watkyn's cooperation, to proceed here and search your room again.

The door flies open and AUNT DAHLIA *rushes in, cow-creamer in hand.*

DAHLIA. Bertie, hide this.

JEEVES (*to the audience*). Ah, dim figure A.

BERTIE. You can't bring that thing in here. Take it away immediately.

DAHLIA. And run into the search party on the stairs! Not if I know it. Have you any ideas, Jeeves?

JEEVES. Not at the moment, madam. I shall see what I can do.

DAHLIA. You can't produce a guilty secret of Sir Watkyn's out of the hat, as you did with Spode?

JEEVES. No, madam.

JEEVES exits.

DAHLIA. We've got to hide the thing somewhere. But where?

BERTIE. Give it to him. (*Pointing at the audience member who has the helmet.*)

DAHLIA. He's already got the helmet.

BERTIE. Oh, yes.

DAHLIA. It's the old problem of course – the one that makes life so tough for murderers – what to do with the body.

BERTIE. Put the bally thing in the suitcase.

DAHLIA. That'll be no good. They're bound to look there.

BERTIE pulls a suitcase from under the bed, and opens it.

BERTIE. True, but I can't stand the sight of it any longer.

He puts the cow-creamer into the suitcase, shuts the lid and forces it into AUNT DAHLIA*'s hands. She tries to hand it back, but* BERTIE *won't touch it. Ultimately* AUNT DAHLIA *upends the case and sits on it, hiding it under her dress.*

DAHLIA. Oh no. That's them coming now.

BERTIE and AUNT DAHLIA *both strike 'innocent' poses. A panic-stricken* GUSSIE *enters.*

BERTIE. Gussie!

GUSSIE. I say, Bertie. A most frightful thing has happened. Sir Watkyn's read the notebook.

BERTIE. What? How on earth did he get hold of the notebook?

GUSSIE. We've just had a row about my newts. He didn't like me putting them in the bath.

BERTIE. You put newts in the bath?

GUSSIE. Yes. I broke the glass tank in my bedroom, that I kept the newts in and the bath was the only place to lodge them.

He went to take a bath. It never occurred to me that anyone would be taking a bath as late as this. And I was in the drawing room, when he burst in shouting: 'Madeline, that blasted Fink-Nottle has been filling my bathtub with tadpoles!' And I lost my head a little, I'm afraid. I yelled: 'Oh, my gosh, you silly old ass, be careful what you're doing with those newts. Don't touch them. I'm in the middle of the most important experiment.'

BERTIE. I see. And then?

GUSSIE. I went on to tell him how I wished to ascertain whether the full moon affected the love life of newts. And a strange look came into his face, and he quivered a bit, and then he told me that he had pulled out the plug and all my newts had gone down the waste pipe. I called him every name I could think of. He broke the wedding off and then I threw the notebook at him for good measure.

BERTIE. Ahh!

BERTIE *falls backwards onto the bed.* GUSSIE *fumbles, unable to figure out where* BERTIE*'s gone.*

GUSSIE. Bertie? Bertie?

DAHLIA. Bertie, I am only a weak woman…

AUNT DAHLIA *slaps* BERTIE *across the face.*

…but if you won't tread on this insect and throw the remains outside, I shall have to see what I can do. The most tremendous issues hanging in the balance and he comes in here, telling us the story of his life. Spink-Bottle, you ghastly goggled-eyed piece of gorgonzola, will you hop it or will you not?

GUSSIE. Yes, Mrs Travers. I'm just going.

DAHLIA. Are you going out of the window?

GUSSIE *pulls a string of knotted sheets from the bed.*

GUSSIE. Yes, Mrs Travers. They do it in books. The moment we get the sheet working, Mrs Travers. If you two tie that end. Then I can borrow Bertie's car and drive to London.

DAHLIA. It's a long drop.

GUSSIE. Oh, not so very, Mrs Travers.

> GUSSIE *throws one end of the string of sheets out of the window and then starts to climb out.*

DAHLIA. You may break your neck.

GUSSIE. Oh, I don't think so.

> GUSSIE *falls from the window.* BERTIE *grabs the end of the string of sheets and attempts* (*without success*) *to pull* GUSSIE *back up again.*

DAHLIA. Come on, Bertie, hurry up.

GUSSIE (*voice-over*). I'm just dangling.

DAHLIA. He's just dangling there.

GUSSIE (*voice-over*). Let me down slowly.

DAHLIA. Let the man down slowly, will you?

GUSSIE (*voice-over*). What are you waiting for?

DAHLIA. What are you waiting for?

> JEEVES *re-enters the room.*

BERTIE. Jeeves!

> BERTIE *lets go of the sheets.*

DAHLIA. Have you come up with a solution, Jeeves?

JEEVES. Yes, if Mr Fink-Nottle is driving your car to London, perhaps he might take your suitcase with him and leave it at the flat.

BERTIE. But, Jeeves, it has the cow-creamer in it.

JEEVES. Precisely, sir.

BERTIE. Jeeves' idea was of such brilliance that I gasped…

> BERTIE *gasps.*

…So did Aunt Dahlia…

AUNT DAHLIA *gasps*.

…I stared at Jeeves…

BERTIE *stares at him*.

…Aunt Dahlia the same…

AUNT DAHLIA *follows suit*.

…And when I dropped the suitcase, it hit Gussie on the head…

GUSSIE *screams*.

…which delighted Aunt Dahlia…

AUNT DAHLIA *sighs delightedly*.

…who then took her leave to see what was going on in the enemy camp.

DAHLIA. I'm going to see what's going on in the enemy camp.

AUNT DAHLIA *exits*.

BERTIE. Well, Jeeves, a short time ago the air was congested with V-shaped depressions, but now one looks north, south, east, and west and describes not a single cloud on the horizon.

JEEVES. Yes, sir. But perhaps the most important piece of news is that Mr Spode has confessed to stealing Constable Oates' helmet.

BERTIE (*to the audience member with the helmet*). You're in the clear!

JEEVES. And he has taken responsibility for all matters. He has even persuaded Sir Watkyn to see the funny side of Mr Fink-Nottle's notebook.

BERTIE. Jeeves! Did you have anything to do with that?

JEEVES. I think I may have influenced his decision by informing him that I knew all about –

BERTIE. Eulalie?

JEEVES. Eulalie. Yes, sir.

BERTIE. Jeeves, you have delivered the goods as seldom before. I'm off the hook, Gussie's getting married and Aunt Dahlia will welcome me back at her dining table. The end of a perfect day, Jeeves.

JEEVES. Thank you, sir. I will finish the packing now.

BERTIE. But, Jeeves, there is just one thing. I do wish you would give me the inside facts about Eulalie. I would keep it dark. You know me – the silent tomb.

JEEVES. The rules of the Junior Ganymede are extremely strict. And there are others present, sir.

BERTIE. Others?

JEEVES *looks out front momentarily.*

I'm sure we can trust them.

JEEVES. That's very generous of you, sir, but I am sorry –

BERTIE. Jeeves, give me the lowdown and… I promise I'll come on that world cruise of yours.

JEEVES. Well, in the strictest confidence, sir –

BERTIE. Of course.

JEEVES. Mr Spode designs ladies' underclothing, sir. He has a considerable talent in that direction, and has indulged it secretly for some years. He is the founder and proprietor of the emporium in Bond Street known as Eulalie Sisters.

BERTIE. Good Lord, Jeeves! No wonder he didn't want a thing like that to come out. You can't be a successful dictator and design women's underclothing. One or other. Not both.

JEEVES. Precisely, sir.

BERTIE. Well, it was worth it, Jeeves. I couldn't have slept wondering about it. Perhaps the cruise won't be so very foul, after all. You'd better get the tickets tomorrow.

JEEVES *coughs.*

JEEVES. I have already procured them, sir. Goodnight.

JEEVES *turns off the main bedroom light and then exits.*

BERTIE. And that's the end of my story.

JEEVES *re-enters.*

JEEVES. Not quite, sir. Your closing speech, sir.

BERTIE. Oh, yes!

JEEVES *snaps his fingers and the entire set starts to disappear, leaving the stage looking exactly as it did at the start of the show.* BERTIE *retrieves the helmet from the audience member and places it on the bed, and then points to another member of the audience.*

BERTIE. Hello up there. I couldn't help noticing that you've been drinking throughout the entire show. I've been to plays like that... You need a bit of help... oh! There were only three of us in the show.

BERTIE *sits down in the armchair.*

BERTIE. Just before the end, Jeeves.

JEEVES. Yes, sir.

BERTIE. There's something I'd like to say, Jeeves.

JEEVES. Yes, sir.

BERTIE. I think I've done pretty well this evening.

JEEVES. You have indeed, sir.

BERTIE. And so have you, Jeeves.

JEEVES. Thank you, sir.

BERTIE. Even you, Seppings.

SEPPINGS. Thank you, sir.

BERTIE. I've had a splendid time.

JEEVES. Your last speech, sir?

BERTIE. Oh, thank you, Jeeves.

JEEVES *stands behind* BERTIE*'s chair.*

BERTIE. The door closed. I switched off the light. For some
moments I lay there on the bed, listening to the measured
tramp of Constable Oates' feet and thinking of Gussie and
Madeline Bassett and of Stiffy and old Stinker Pinker, and of
the hotsy-totsiness which now prevailed in their love lives. I
also thought of Uncle Tom being handed the cow-creamer.

And presently the eyes closed, the muscles relaxed, the
breathing became soft and regular, and sleep which does
something which has slipped my mind to the something
sleave of care poured over me in a healing wave.

BERTIE. Do we have to do this all over again tomorrow,
Jeeves?

JEEVES. I'm afraid so, sir.

SEPPINGS *comes on to switch the power off.*

Blackout.

The End.

*The curtain call of the original production evolved into a
comically choreographed Charleston routine.*

www.nickhernbooks.co.uk

facebook.com/nickhernbooks

twitter.com/nickhernbooks